ALIGNING THE GLACIER'S GHOST

RIVER TEETH LITERARY NONFICTION PRIZE
Daniel Lehman and Joe Mackall, Series Editors

The River Teeth Literary Nonfiction Prize is awarded to the best work of literary nonfiction submitted to the annual contest sponsored by *River Teeth: A Journal of Nonfiction Narrative*.

Also available in the River Teeth Literary Nonfiction Prize:

Disequilibria: Meditations on Missingness by Robert Lunday
What Cannot Be Undone: True Stories of a Life in Medicine by Walter M. Robinson
The Rock Cycle: Essays by Kevin Honold
Try to Get Lost: Essays on Travel and Place by Joan Frank
I Am a Stranger Here Myself by Debra Gwartney
MINE: Essays by Sarah Viren
Rough Crossing: An Alaskan Fisherwoman's Memoir by Rosemary McGuire
The Girls in My Town: Essays by Angela Morales

ALIGNING THE GLACIER'S GHOST

Essays on Solitude and Landscape

Sarah Capdeville

UNIVERSITY OF NEW MEXICO PRESS

ALBUQUERQUE

Printed in the United States of America

ISBN 978-0-8263-6593-4 (paper)
ISBN 978-0-8263-6594-1 (ePub)
Library of Congress Cataloging-in-Publication data is on file with the Library of Congress.

Founded in 1889, the University of New Mexico sits on the traditional homelands of the Pueblo of Sandia. The original peoples of New Mexico—Pueblo, Navajo, and Apache—since time immemorial have deep connections to the land and have made significant contributions to the broader community statewide. We honor the land itself and those who remain stewards of this land throughout the generations and also acknowledge our committed relationship to Indigenous peoples. We gratefully recognize our history.

Cover photographs by Isaac Morris and Danny Savage
Designed by Isaac Morris
Composed in Charter, Flood, and Malaga

Contents

Part I

SWITCHBACK

1. Carve Away the Moon 3
2. Exposure 17
3. Places to Avoid at Dusk 31
4. Siento 37
5. Headwater 50
6. Stories That Hold Water 58

Part II

POINT OF RETURN

7. Porcupine Ridge 75
8. Different Kinds of Solitude 82
9. What Stones Hold 95
10. Cracking the Window 109
11. Reasons to Carry Bear Spray 123
12. The Long View 130

Acknowledgments 145
References 147

PART I

SWITCHBACK

1

Carve Away the Moon

Somewhere on a peninsula of pine and birch a hundred miles north of the Arctic Circle, there's a velvet-green pasture, a square of green that breaks the snatch of cloudberry and bog and reeds marching inland from a lake touching sky. This is where my mind slips to, one place of too many, in the weeks after I find a lump in my right breast.

I remember the ruts in the muddy track splitting back into the birch, the foreign feel of that grass in a place that shrugs away attempts at agriculture. I remember standing in the middle of the field, hushed of wind and breath, how it felt like the eye of a storm. Sometimes I remember a slope-beamed barn abandoned at its center, and sometimes I can't recall if there was anything but green there at all.

Here in the Rockies, August bleeds past, warm wind and deep green maples and the cottonwoods across the street long rid of their tufted seeds. The present blurs, trips over itself. Memory swells, fills the gaps like pitch to a borehole.

Reality snaps—my doctor's eyes widening as she feels the lump, only for a second, only enough time to scrape professionalism away from surprise. My mind is desperate to escape this moment, the brush of fingers against a wrongness under my skin, the hard *c* stuck in the back of my throat. I think of a timbered ridge south of my hometown where a goshawk once sharpened her talons on the air above my temple, how I tucked my chin to my chest and sprinted, blundered, fled that small and deliberate danger.

•

The lump on the ultrasound monitor takes the form of an oblong moon. The radiologist points out the muscles of my chest below, tight waves of a prairie horizon. The fact that the lump rests parallel to the layers of my chest is a good indication, he says. It doesn't throw a shadow across the rest of the tissue. "Anything cancerous usually sucks resources and we see a blurry dark spot," he says. And there's the word, gaping as the moon rising full over my ribs.

Once I climbed a small butte with a friend to watch a total solar eclipse. The red-quartz rock around us paled, air tinged with the coolness of a sudden dusk. I watched my own shadow disappear, held my hands in front of me as they turned a quiet gray. The sky, that cloudless afternoon, swallowed itself. The horizon, hemmed in pine and sagebrush, flared green and then dark.

What I didn't know about solar eclipses was that the moon is entirely absent until the moment it carves into the sun. No cratered scythe ebbing in the blue, no snowy thumbprint trailing our sun. Nothing but a body hiding in its own shadow.

"You can keep an eye on it and check back in six months," the radiologist tells me. "Or you can get a biopsy and know for sure." He wipes the ultrasound gel from my skin, the same cool and silent breeze.

•

In 1935 an Austrian-Irish physicist named Erwin Schrödinger grew frustrated with an interpretation of quantum physics where a particle like an atom or photon exists in multiple states until it is observed. To point out the slick slope of this angle, he came up with a thought experiment in which a cat is locked in a box along with a beacon of poison released only if a sensor detects radioactivity. There is also a single radioactive atom in the hypothetical box.

If, Schrödinger argued, what later came to be known as the Copenhagen interpretation of quantum mechanics were true, then the atom would be in a state of both decay and stability. There would be both radioactivity and no radioactivity. The sensor would trip as well as stay still. Poison would spill fumes into the box and also remain contained. The cat would be both dead and alive. Until someone opens the box.

Most people don't recognize Schrödinger's cat as an experiment of absurdity. Most people don't trace it back to theories of superpositions or entanglements or macroscopic states, but rather cling to this idea of observation, of knowing and unknowing. Inside a box is a cat, and the cat's state of being is unknowable until we see it. It's a familiar feeling, superpositions not of minute particles but of whole, twisted, lopsided, charged outcomes in life—a college admissions envelope, a wrapped gift, a crush of unknown reciprocity, a weighted phone call, a test result.

I think of all the times I've hesitated or been forced to hesitate in front of a closed container, wonder if Erwin Schrödinger would be angry at the misinterpretation of his thought experiment created to expose a misinterpretation. I think of the times I've broken or dropped or otherwise altered something—a bowl on the kitchen floor, a folder of organized files, an ankle popping under my weight—and looked away, as if that would change the outcome, as if the outcome could stay suspended, unknown, unmarked until I had the capacity to bear witness. I wonder if, in making a point about the ridiculousness of a theory on the smallest of scales, Schrödinger ever considered how much it spoke to something so much bigger, and so less defined.

•

The lump is the size of a peach stone. I can't think of it any other way, because the day before I found it, my partner and I drove out of town to car camp for a night, and I ate a peach while perched in the camp chair, biting the sweet pulp down to its ribbed pit. Late summer sunlight pockmarked the still water of the pond below us, and as the evening deepened, the gray edge of sky ruffled into thunderheads. My dog knew best, butt-tucking to the tent that she all but dug herself into, and we followed, soon holding water bottles up to the drips of downpour pulsing through the tent seams.

I remember the drum of that sudden rain, the smell of midsummer dirt churned to mud. I remember the open-air Jeeps and rust-speckled pickups of the locals at the pond below, the scream of a chainsaw from someone cutting wood just for the fun of it. I want to remember what I did with the peach pit, because now it feels like a hollow in time, a hardness snapped from one flesh to another.

•

I choose the biopsy.

A week smudges past, and then I'm back at the hospital, stiff gown open to the front. The radiologist explains the process—numb the area with lidocaine, then use a hollow biopsy needle to make three or four passes through the mass. The needle and apparatus rest on a tray beside him under a sterile drape the color of open sky at high noon, as if hiding them from view will dull the reason I'm here.

Above the exam table is a wide monitor hooked up to the ultrasound wand that the radiologist is using to visualize the lump. He asks me if I want it left on, and I nod, though later I'll regret the decision, regret the imaging of those barbs—first the small prick of lidocaine, then the core biopsy needle—into the horizons of my body. I'll want the blue drape back, think of the deep green field in Lapland without any barn in its center, without any splinters wormed into its earth.

There's no pain but an intensity of pressure, the radiologist pushing the ultrasound wand against one side of my breast and forcing the needle in from the other, which I will later learn is a 12 gauge. I'm shocked at the density of the tissue, how much strength I can see the radiologist putting into the effort, how much my body is resisting even the sharpest of edges.

"The biopsy needle is quite loud," the radiologist warns me. And it is, a jarring clack that reminds me of the heavy-duty staple guns I used to post signs as a wilderness ranger. I feel the repercussions shoot through my torso, an earthquake to my guts. Above on the screen the biopsy needle hovers on the outer edge of the mass, and the radiologist inserts another sample core, pulls what I imagine is a trigger. The needle bucks forward, pierces the gray and speckled moon.

In college, for an ecology course, I once cored a tree, a stately ponderosa pine up a canyon that now I frequently hike. It felt wrong at first, twisting the borer through sweet and dry bark, puzzle pieces that flaked away with the wind, and into the tree's cambium, its living layer, soft and almost tempting to bite. I kept twisting the corer, wrist clicking like a nuthatch, until my knuckles touched the rough bark, until the core broke from the rest of its body. Coaxed out, it was like a banded pencil, and I stood there beside the trunk, air sharp with the pitch of that injury, marveling at how easily lines of drought and snowmelt can turn into memory.

I remember the time, as a wilderness ranger, that my crew and I crosscut-sawed through a massive tamarack tumbled earthbound across the trail, its wood the closest to hardwood I've ever worked through. How after we'd shoved the round off the tread, I sat with my shoulder against the freshly sawed trunk, counting every ring to its core—208 years from seedling to canopy, 208 bands between germination and that massive shadow groaning, cracking, pinching, toppling down.

•

There are photos of me during this time, and in every one I'm surprised at the normalcy in my face, the genuine smile as I pick huckleberries or split wood in the backyard, recklessly barefoot. I remind myself that it's our nature to mask, to cover up, and that two things can exist at once, that joy under late-summer sunshine alongside the gnawing unknown under my shirt.

Right there, I want to say, pointing at my chest, but really I mean *right there*, in my eyes, as if the pupil might eclipse, as if the fear, green as June alfalfa, might glint like metal among the blue.

•

Doctors aren't supposed to promise anything. But mine did, at least the radiologist who did the first imaging of the mass—that a biopsy would be an answer. And he was wrong to promise, because the biopsy, like the ultrasound, comes back inconclusive, pathologists frowning in their observation of my cells under the microscope. The next step, a second radiologist tells me over the phone, his words tightly wrapped to avoid the same mistake of the first, is surgery, a biopsy lumpectomy.

My voice gums in my throat, a chill creeping up from the souls of my feet—that shock of cool water at the reservoir outside town that my friends and I would visit every summer. Sometimes we'd leave the windows cranked shut on the drive over, so that by the time we waded in the water would be a welcome rush, but no matter how sticky our skin or flushed our cheeks, that deep, dammed body was always a shock, always a chill to fumble past.

The reservoir was once a canyon, a gathering place. There had even been a town down there, its cemetery staked higher on a hillside that's now an island, so that now all that's left of the town are the memorials of its dead.

The coming winter my dad and some friends will camp overnight on the island, will haul their packs and firewood on sleds a mile out onto the ice before gleams of blue sky turn to heavy snow squalls. In the morning, my dad will tell me, they woke to coyote prints ringing the island, hundreds of them on the perfect canvas of grainy snow atop ice, as if they had been in search of something all night, never once making a sound, even as a full moon glossed the frozen world.

•

The core biopsy needle made four spring-loaded passes through the mass, and when the radiologist withdrew it, I felt a spill of warm blood down my side. Now, in the mirror, the bruising shadows the lump that was once invisible under my skin. It's an alpine lake, gunmetal blue, the same body of water printed over and over on all the topographic maps I've collected, hitched to gravity by a single veined outlet, dark and valley bound.

It could be any lake, I think, tucked against talus blooming with geraniums, bluebells, paintbrush. Sunset gold tamaracks gilding its reflection, or the smooth bones of whitebark snags. It could be the morning I watched a single cow elk step into a misted shore to drink, her sawdust-brown calf trotting in behind her, breaking the milky pane of the water with his youth. The cow elk huffed—at the calf, at the exposure of the still blue lake, at me, seated and still on its opposite shore. I know she saw me, or at least smelled me, our awareness of each other like one long line across the water, pinned to either shore.

She drank one last time, then lifted her head skyward that way only elk do, as if they're swimming through air. Huffed at her calf, still innocent of my presence, who tossed his head, so small for his muscled body, and loped after her. I watched one flash of their umber coats through the wall of fir and spruce, and then they were gone. I continued to sit, still, waiting for the ripples of their passage to yawn across the lake.

•

This, I think, is what people mean when they say their life flashes before their eyes. Maybe not the acute moment, world tipped upside down on a fractured windshield, dark mouth of a gun in a grocery store. But a drawn out tumble, a string of all the wrong answers. This is, I tell myself, my mind grappling for comfort where the present offers none, where the present is hushed in snowfall from the cottonwoods across the street but still, painfully, the phone rings from the cancer care nurses, who still, painfully, refuse to say that word except when introducing themselves. When I ask what if the lump is malignant, the question becomes the goshawk, and I'm told to tuck my head and keep rushing forward.

So I stop where I can—the monthly astronomy lectures my family went to at the local college, lecture hall lights dimmed so that the professor's images of stars and nebulae and ice-capped moons flashed in the dark. For an hour I would try and understand space and time and gravity, try and grasp the enormity of our galaxy twisting around itself or the physics of black holes, how a shadow can be so weighted that it warps even light. And at the end of the talk, the professor would flick the lights back on, and that dark, complex world beyond our atmosphere would pale to flecks on the projector screen, and we'd all file outside, into the only world we knew, where the sun had just broken like a yolk behind the horizon and the first stars sparked overhead, bodies that would never swallow us in our lifetimes.

Or, I think, maybe those lectures were never held in summer, because paired with that spilled sunset are memories of coats and scarves crammed between the folding seats, of us shuffling outside over ice sparked with gravel, night one long shadow across the parking lot. Maybe my mind is so desperate to flick the lights back on that it's mixing memories, mixing metaphors, warping this summer into a black hole of its own.

•

The lumpectomy's purpose is to determine if the mass in my breast is a common fibroadenoma, less likely given its lack of diagnosis by both ultrasound and biopsy, or a rarer phyllodes tumor, and if so whether it's benign, borderline, or malignant. I do the thing you're not supposed to do and open far too many tabs on my internet browser—Mayo

Clinic, Breastcancer.org, American Cancer Society, Johns Hopkins. Most phyllodes tumors are benign, I read, but if they are cancerous, they're notoriously difficult to treat because they form in the connective tissue. Chemotherapy and radiation aren't as effective treatments. I tell myself I'm ignoring this fact.

I trace the word *phyllodes* back to its Greek root, *phullon*, which means leaflike. Under the microscope, cells of phyllodes tumors are said to warp and bend and stretch like deciduous leaves. I squint these images of violet- and pink-stained cells, knots of flattened tissue and beads of nuclei but, no matter how hard I try, I can't see the cells as leaves. They have no form, no metaphor or simile or look-alike to pin an understanding. The cells cluster and widen and push and stretch and encircle. They are a landscape I don't know how to cross.

•

The week of the surgery, wildfires on the West Coast snarl in size and intensity, and all that smoke moves inland like crumpled sandpaper. One morning I watch the sun come up over the ridge to the northeast, a low ember fumbling up silhouettes of pines like a dark orange bulb. The smoke sifts into the valley, an endless dusk and constant need to clear my throat.

I think of the time I flew to the coast to meet my friend to watch the solar eclipse, how there was a hot and deadly fire burning in my home mountains then. Big fires like that break through layers of the atmosphere, plumes of soot and grit and heat pushing through the upper troposphere into the stratosphere, sometimes higher than the cruising altitude of passenger planes. That afternoon as my plane arched over the Rockies, we hit turbulence not from a low pressure system, but from the fires burning below.

The plane bumped over the smoke, cabin floor rattling. I felt the texture of the plumes in the soles of my feet, like a ram butting his head against the plane's belly, pictured all the material burned and hollowed and seared and gusted ten or twenty thousand feet into the atmosphere—sprigs of beargrass, chips of bark, splinters from someone's woodshed, pine needles like rice paper, ash as fine as rubbed sage.

One night I dream that I'm wheeled into the operating room, which is dark and spotlit and cold. The moment the anesthesiologist presses the mask to my face in the dream, I start to wake up, so that sleep paralysis intersects with the false paralysis of that imagined anesthesia. Everything tips upside down. In the fading dream I cling to a consciousness that doesn't exist, buck my body against an operating table that is my own bed, that doesn't yield either way. I'm awake enough to feel the terror, unconscious enough to still be seeped in the chill of the dim room. Muscles snuffed from flight, diaphragm like cracked slate under my lungs.

My head floods—like rising out of dark water into glinting air, that moment when underwater is airborne, cupped against straining eardrums, until wind curls and breaks that barrier, and the oxygenated world rushes back in. Movement snaps back into my body. My heart beats in fits. The yellow sun and hard-edged moon, locked at the exact right moment, continue to scrape apart.

•

I had a professor in grad school who said that we remember certain things for a reason. Not that everything happens for a reason, but that our brains shuffle short-term memories to fixed long-term ones because there's something important, essential, sublime about them, that they're the ones worth holding on to.

I don't know why I can recall the routes to mountain peaks I've only touched once but can't remember yesterday. Outside is a mirror, gritty haze that turns the air strangely cool and dry for early September. My partner takes a photo of me sitting on the couch in a wool beanie and crewneck, a down blanket over my lap, smiling even though on the other side of that smoke I can't take a full breath.

Here is the rattle of adrenaline under the goshawk's talons, the chalky feel of a rock wall in Rome, the time my mom and I visited a sled dog kennel in the valley of the Little Blackfoot and ate Girl Scout cookies in dripping March sun. Here is the rutted road that shoulders out of pine and spruce into the green, square meadow, all velvet grass and thin clouds overhead, mosquitoes humming up from the marshes in a time and place where the sky never tips towards dusk, where the sun circles and circles and circles but never throws that meadow into night. Here is the cat in a steel box, waiting.

•

Unlike the dream, I don't remember the surgery. The last thing I remember is the cold plastic mask over my nose and mouth, its hiss of air damp and cool as mist over alpine water. The events prior stack backwards like a skipping stone, slaps of hard memory and whooshed gaps. The sedation drugs—dexmedetomidine and propofol—don't just blur time, but snatch whole chunks, bleeding their haze backwards. I can remember being rolled into the cold brightness of the operating room, but only slivers of my gowned shuffle from the inpatient bed to the table. I see the instrument tray, draped in that same pale blue; whether or not the scalpels and blades flash under the gaudy fluorescent lights is snuffed out.

Back still, the chilled seep of antianxiety medication into my IV, a steady stream of kind and purposed nurses, including the one who found a vein her first prick. My surgeon frowning at her clipboard at the nurses' station, as if one of us has gotten the date wrong, before she strides in to uncap a Sharpie from her coat pocket and draw two possible incision lines on my breast, scribbling her initials there too. The anesthesiologist, kind eyes and soft-spoken in the midst of all the echoes of medical jargon and assurances and beds wheeling past. Another nurse tasked with finagling the cords that plug into the pneumatic compression devices around my calves, until he finally gets the machine to coordinate with the devices and they squeeze and release, squeeze and release, squeeze and release my legs until my ankles go numb.

When I was a kid my family would drive out onto the Rocky Mountain Front, the high plains rolling into yellowed bluffs lipped by still-winged hawks, then turn back west into mountains that rose like long fortresses. We made this trip a couple times throughout my childhood, always in late August or September when the bugs had mostly died off, with our family dog Victor, a border collie and heeler mix whose coat was patched the same color as the plains.

The trail of the hike coiled against the Dearborn River, which I remember always running fast and full, even in late summer. The river thundered through polished bends of deep-sienna rock, braided into whitewater by shelved boulders. We played in the water where the currents were slow, sometimes sprinted in for a full-body dip.

One year, going too far into the rapids to fetch a stick or just underestimating the sweep of strong currents below the surface, Victor was pulled out into the rapids. I don't know if I saw him slip into the water, white fur of his coat blending into the spume, but I do remember him clambering onto one of the boulders in the middle of the river, long collie tail ribboned in water and pinned to the underside of his belly. Even now, I can see him shuffle his front paws back and forth on the umber stone, surrounded on all sides by heaving snowmelt and fine mist, can still hear his yelps, jarring as fresh blood, over the river's continual bellow.

What I don't remember is how our family dog made it back to the pebbled riverbank. The memory splits and roils—my dad recklessly wading into an eddy, or Victor leaping into a chute as glossed as sea glass—all loud and jumbled and soaked in helplessness, a dull hammer against my chest. One moment Victor was a wet, crying tremble on that solitary island, and then he was there with us, shaking his own mist, jostled but just fine, relief evaporating off all five of us. What I do know is that at some point while he teetered on that refuge of carved stone, I turned around, or walked away, because I couldn't watch whatever happened, because the hammer on my chest had become an ax, and if I didn't run it would carve my own heart right out.

When I wake from the surgery, vision too blurred to do any good, my first impulse is to touch my chest. A nurse's gentle hands move my fingers away, assures me that no, there was no need to put any drains in. My bladder, sodden with IV fluids, demands release. The surgeon smudges into frame and then is gone, along with whatever she said. In the outpatient bed, I pinch my eyes shut to the eddying world and sob, ax flipped to its flat-faced poll and swinging hard nevertheless.

•

The first thing I do after my partner drives me home from the hospital is shuffle into the bathtub. I'm not allowed to remove my bandages or get anything close to the incision site wet for two more days, but I turn on the faucet and soap my legs where the pneumatic compression devices hummed away clots, my arms where the IV site throbs and has already started to bloom into a bruise, my hair with its smell of Betadine and sterile cloth. The anesthetics pitch gravity, turn the bathtub into a slick canyon.

Mostly I want to scrub away the moments I don't remember, the gaps of time under the skipping stone, under the dome lights, under the knife. All these strangers over my body, lifting and holding my arms away from my chest, and boring into it, snipping horizons, digging through thunderheads to carve away the moon.

•

The surgeon told me that she'd get the results back from pathology within two or three days. Three days pass and I don't hear anything. I call the office; no, nothing is back yet. I call the next day, and a nurse tells me the results are in, and my surgeon will give me a call later that day. She doesn't.

•

When I look back at photos of myself from this summer, there's one I regret never taking. After the required seventy-two hours, I slowly unwind the bandaging from my body in front of the bathroom mirror.

The bruising fans out like an oil spill, broader than my handspan, and over the next days and weeks will turn colors I didn't know possible for the body—a rainstorm grating against sunset, smoke from burning willow, deep red hoods of long-rusted Model Ts flecking away in abandoned gulches, yellowed grass submerged under high spring runoff, sharp green of new tamarack needles. A tail of pooled blood laps against my ribs, blue as preemptive dusk.

I think I will always remember the colors. Still, memory is a slick slope of evidence.

•

Explaining his thought experiment, Erwin Schrödinger wrote, "It is typical of these cases that an indeterminacy originally restricted to the atomic domain becomes transformed into macroscopic indeterminacy, which can then be *resolved* by direct observation. That prevents us from so naïvely accepting as valid a 'blurred model' for representing reality. In itself, it would not embody anything unclear or contradictory," he concluded. "There is a difference between a shaky or out-of-focus photograph and a snapshot of clouds and fog banks."

•

When the surgeon calls on a Friday evening, I'm sitting on the back porch in the rocking chair my partner and I painted sky blue with sunny balsamroots that spring. Or maybe I'm sitting in the cracked plastic Adirondack chair that somehow supports my hips better. I don't remember. The smoke-cast sky leans heavy on the backyard trees, their leaves like palms asking for rain, and I am sitting, waiting.

The mass is a phyllodes tumor and benign, the surgeon tells me. "Clear margins, nothing to worry about," she says brightly, as if she'd fixed a leaking sink. As if I haven't already lived the hypothetical in my head too many times to count, as if it weren't a stone deep in my throat, a cracked shell spilling runners into my mouth, leaves as soft as dawn unfurling against my tongue.

"Have a great weekend," she tells me, and hangs up.

•

I sit in the rocking chair or the Adirondack chair, still. Stare at the low curtains of green, the high gray haze woven of a million tiny things that were once whole, wet, rooted.

In my chest now there is a hollow knotted with scars. Later, clipping the ties of my sutures, the surgeon will tell me to become familiar with how the scar tissue feels, so that if the tumor comes back, I can tell them apart. Which is to say—learn the shape of memory, what the body fills in absence, how wounding is an edge that throws us into dusk whether or not it's noticed.

I picture a cross section of the mass, like a crosscut tree, under the microscope, about the words the pathologist typed. I think about the solar eclipse, how the moon was nonexistent until its shadow arced hard and dark into the sun. I think about the green meadow in Lapland, about the churning snowmelt of the Dearborn and our dog stranded in its throat and trotting its banks, the town submerged under planks of ice save for its tombstones, about the tamarack with its 208 rings of growth and that oldest rhetorical question—*If a tree falls in the woods and no one is around to hear it, does it really make a sound?* And I realize, slowly, that it's all the same question as whether Schrödinger's cat is dead or alive, which is only another way of asking how, in the mess of this world, we are supposed to bear witness.

Shadows murmur into clefts in the hillsides. Somewhere a coyote sings a plume against moonlight. Rain turns to snow on the branches of an old pine, cracked in scabs of a lightning strike. Somewhere else a peach tree grows where it belongs. An elk follows a worn path to water. The sun sinks, finally, behind the tree line of a green meadow, and I remember it all.

2

Exposure

Five thousand feet above rocky cuts of mountain and slopes softened by the creep of whortleberry, Froze-to-Death Plateau opens into a taut palm, its name a promise of exposure. Ridged fingers reach back into the heavy blue waters of alpine lakes. Up here the air moves as a different breed of wind—not the gusts strumming stands of lodgepole below, or a warm hush over the plains to the east, but a rough breeze that sidles against sky and takes advice from the jet stream. On this steadily rising table of the Beartooth Mountains, carpets of green fade—hardy willow to low clumps of sedges to loose talus the color of copper to, at the plateau's thumb, the slow crumble of earth, great gray stones harboring pockets of yesterday's summer snowfall.

In all my ramblings, I've never seen so much sky or land or color. I've never felt so small in a place, and it's not because of the plateau's enormity. It's because of its openness. Against the severity of the plateau's ravines and cliffs where it sloughs away, against the sharpness of iron-stained stones and pink geraniums and sky that sings pure, indescribable blue, I've never felt such an absence of edges.

•

A Vivaldi sonata trickles through the waiting room. It's a catch of calm I leave with reluctance as I step into the therapist's office, my eyes immediately finding the window on the opposite wall. Autumn flits maple and oak leaves across the streets. I sit down on the couch, squinting at the wash of natural light and lamps in the room. It already feels like the wrong place on the couch to sit, the wrong room, the wrong decision to come here.

The therapist has already asked, too many times, how I am, and I don't know what answer she wants. I've only just gotten here, only just sat down. She watches me with eyebrows swooped up in consideration. The silence of the room is a vast space I can't fill.

"So," she says. "What can I help you with?"

The answer, for simplicity's sake, is that I promised a friend I'd come here. I'd been on the phone with her a week ago spiraling into a black pit of paralysis, forehead pressed into my knees, words swallowing themselves until I couldn't speak or move.

I fold my legs again and let my fingers grasp each other. Anxiety, I tell her, response rehearsed. An easy reply, a simple label. The *what* is uncomplicated. It's harder to poke at the bedrock of my choice to schedule this appointment, the *why*.

The therapist tilts her head. "You seem to be handling it well," she says, as if I should take her words as a compliment, as if she believes this is something I desperately need to hear. "You look pretty composed on the outside," she adds.

That, I think, is the entire reason I'm here.

•

I've given up running with pepper spray whenever I'm back in my hometown of Helena. I'm never without a canister in grizzly country, but there are only a scattering of shy black bears here. Mostly, the main predators are mountain lions. And for a mountain lion the plume of protection from pepper spray offers just a false peace of mind. A lion is a stealth predator, relying on the silence of her wide paws across a bed of pine needles. It's why whitetail deer wag high tufted tails like flags when they run. *You've been spotted*, they're saying to the predator crouched behind a screen of juniper. *You can't sneak up on me anymore.*

I've searched the ebony eyes of deer for anxiety. Both of us jolt at loud noises, take note of exits, prefer greenery to asphalt. But the deer knows what she's running from. There's a theory that anxiety in people stems from the relative ease of our modern lives—no lions pacing the perimeters of our homes, so our brains overreact, spooling terror into a terrorless void. Still, with all the time I've spent in the backcountry, saturated in the real possibility of bear attacks and broken bones and heat stroke, I can say anxiety doesn't care if there's a real threat or not. Not to mention exposure to those dangers doesn't dampen its hold.

Spotting a mountain lion means she's only circling in curiosity or inexperience. Cougar attacks come from behind—unannounced, unspoken, a clutch of canines effective and instant. There's no time to release a cloud of stinging aerosol.

I've never seen a mountain lion in the wild, only the marks of her passage. Imprint of her long tail swiped in fresh snow like a watercolor brush void of paint. The knead of her claws on a deer carcass, hair ripped from hide and spat into a halo around tendon and bone.

Sometimes, running in Helena's South Hills, I stop in my tracks, snagged by the presence of a soft ebb on the back of my neck. I spin around, holding my breath to the stillness.

The chickadees and juncos fall silent too. This is what it feels like to be watched.

•

One Halloween growing up, I dressed up as a die. After gluing panels of white poster board together, my dad helped me cut a hole in the bottom of the box for my legs, a smaller one on top where my head poked out. He lined the top hole with gray pipe insulation so the edges wouldn't grate into my neck.

We glued black dots to the sides and made one into a flap from which I could thrust out my right hand for candy. Inside the die it was comforting, a dim cubical cloak that went from neck to mid-thigh. If I wiggled around enough I could pull myself into the interior of soft white edges, disappearing altogether.

That year, late October brought a cold snap of temperatures flirting with zero. Suddenly a Halloween of scampering across dark lawns in mismatched stages of dress didn't seem like a good idea, and we loaded my die into the back of our Jeep. Our mom drove my brother and me to the Catholic college in town, where students were handing out candy from dorm rooms in response to the cold snap and parents worrying about frostbite.

Praise and mock surprise spilled out of doorways in the overpacked refuge. The hallways eddied and surged with Jedi masters, forest creatures, cowgirls, wizards, dinosaurs, sports stars, firemen.

And me in the middle, a plodding wide box bumping into other kids, thumping into fire extinguishers clamped to the walls, wishing more and more I hadn't come.

I never felt drawn to Halloween like my friends, who spent most of October brainstorming costume ideas. All that candy made my stomach cramp, and I dreaded being the source of observation. I was one of those kids desperate for acknowledgement and terrified of inquiry. Sensitive to loud noises, I opted out of most haunted houses, and given the chance to participate in their production, I liked to crouch under tables, out of sight, snatching at people's ankles.

But I loved the die costume so much that the next year I repurposed it into a present, taping its sides with a roll of glossy scarlet wrapping paper, a big bow stuck to one corner. The weather was more reasonable that fall, and I got to roam with a group of friends across lawns, back into the shelter of outside. I grinned in doorways, endowed with a rare sense of confidence.

"You're a present," whoever opened the door would say, and I'd nod in enthusiastic relief. They never asked the question I dreaded, always dread, never asked me to pull back layers of wrapping paper and black construction paper and poster board to where I hugged my knees in a hushed recess. They never asked who I was.

•

On the summit of Ben Nevis, the highest mountain in the United Kingdom, I bury my camera into the inner pocket of my jacket and press fingers into my armpits. Both are nearly frozen. In my rush to leave behind the groups of boisterous English families threading the switchbacked trail below, I arrived up here breathing hard, warmth flooding out from my core. Wind cleaves heat away from my extremities, and for a minute I don't mind taking in the view as is.

Hills painted in moss and heather stretch into the glen bottoms below, gleaming in sunlight that wanders south. Valleys open like folds of cotton. There's no sound except the wind swallowing the mountaintop, and it tears at my clothes and snatches at my numb-blushed face. Clouds skirt through the glens below and crowd white paws against the mountains long ago sculpted by glaciers, weaving and huddling and leaping with tufted chests into the air. They catch in the booming wind, and suddenly the view is smeared away.

My vision clouds white, but I can wait. Another throttle of wind shoves the fog away, and sunlight pours color back into place. To the east, salty fingers of lochs weave into the highlands. I squint, trying to make out the isle I came from yesterday, a strip of stone in dark waters. From up here roads and waterways stretch like features on a map, lines of definition I can trace from a distance. Below I navigate the thick of it. Too often people ask where I'm headed, and half the time I don't know myself.

At Ben Nevis's base, weaving back down through group after group of visitors, I stick out my thumb from the roadside. It's the first time I've ever hitchhiked, and the first car to pass, a sleek silver compact, stops for me.

"Fort William?" I ask the driver, which is just down the glen, where I can catch a bus back to that sliver of limestone. It's a future I can hold onto, the name of a place.

The driver nods and waves me in, but he's also picked up my accent. As we coast down the road hemmed in amber rowan trees, I tell him where I've come from—Montana. I'm recently graduated from college, spending all the money I earned the previous summer working in the Absaroka-Beartooth Wilderness to backpack across Europe as I figure out what I'm doing next. It's the first of a handful of quarter-life crises.

The interior of the car smells fresh and looks like someone vacuums it every morning. I glance at my muddy shoes, knuckles cracked from Ben Nevis's wind-shaken summit. My hair is frizzed into disarray, and I can make out the stale smell of sweat wafting from my jacket.

Suddenly I see this trope, this character I've become, some young woman in a Jack Kerouac novel if he actually wrote multidimensional women, a disillusioned copy of Cheryl Strayed or Elizabeth Gilbert, searching for epiphany at the world's highest points. It's not like that, I tell myself. I swear.

I stare out the sideview mirror, back towards the gray rise of Ben Nevis, now settling into a white wall of clouds.

•

When I was little, my father tells me, I would dip into a subdued silence that sometimes broke into tears. I was a sensitive kid, and found the world full of sharp edges.

"What's wrong?" my dad would ask.

And I would reply, "Anything."

•

Diethyltoluamide. My mouth tumbles over its pronunciation; it's by far easier to just say DEET. Out here, my speech flows easily through *kinnikinnick, thimbleberry, tamarack*. But this green bottle of eighty percent DEET insect repellant with too many words in all caps glares with its chemicals.

I stand in my Forest Service uniform and look back up at the subalpine fir crashed across the tread, bug spray in my palm. It's been a plague of windstorms flattening dead trees across the Rattlesnake all spring, and my two interns are already fed up with the trail clearing, sawing tree after fallen tree. They don't seem to share my love of the crosscut saw.

I wave a speckled cloud of mosquitoes out of my vision. Ahead on the trail, more logs tangle across the tread, some live and soft, others dead and brittle, all spanning this wet pocket of greenery humming with bugs keen on our blood. We'll surely be spending a good two hours here, moving only our arms back and forth with the slice of the saw.

My skin is already sticky with sweat and sunscreen, and like the surrounding leaves of Rocky Mountain maple and huckleberry brushes, I know it's permeable. The diethyltoluamide, with all its complex synthetic chains, will soak into my roots. So like every day that season, I pass on the bug repellent. I clasp my handle of the crosscut saw and start pulling, shaking my head like a gnat-plagued mare.

The mosquitos and black flies keep lifting from the brush and swarm, overjoyed at my hippie conduct. Sometimes they're brash, buzzing at my eyes and forehead, but the clever ones find stealthy places to bite, always the back of something. The back of my legs, the back of my arms, behind my ears.

This is the worst place. When I get back from this hitch, that ridge of bone behind my left ear swells so much I can't fully turn my head.

Welts and bumps pepper my legs and hairline, but in the shower, I only wash away the grit of the backcountry, no DEET spiraling down the drain. Just sweat and mud and clumped webs from spiders and budworms. The occasional boxwood leaf, a sprinkle of fir needles, strands of wolf's mane lichen. Lines of dirt congregate like freckles on my forearm, a mark of my body I'll be reluctant to scrub away for months.

In front of the mirror, I twist my head and peer at the damage from the black flies, flinching. I step back and stare at myself as a whole. Brown hair curled from swims in alpine lakes, cheeks flushed with sunburn and dry heat. Shoulders and biceps toned from all those hours pulling the crosscut back and forth, back and forth. I flex my arms at my reflection. Despite the stubborn grime and sunburn and bug bites quadrupled by stubbornness, I find that rare jewel of liking what I see.

•

The Finnish village of Inari stands as a collection of lackluster buildings and unnerving number of parking lots. Herds of reindeer click wide hooves across the asphalt. Up the brushy bank from the lakeshore, there's a small stand where a man sells trout crisp and wrapped in aluminum foil. The village grocery store sits one parking lot back from the town's main road, which goes either south for fifty kilometers to Ivalo, the closest airport, or north towards the cookie-cutter coast of Norway. Up there, edging towards the Barents Sea, the forest knows it's running out of land. Pines and spruce drop away to stubby birchwood and mosquito-choked bogs.

Inside the grocery store I hold a cup of yogurt in my palm, trying to decipher the long string of letters on its label. In Finland some foods are also branded in Norwegian and Swedish, languages of Germanic origin, which is one step closer to comprehension to me. Finnish is an island language, unrelated to its neighbors. The words under the image of a pale spoonful of yogurt aren't helping me at all.

After a semester studying abroad in Spain, I'm working at a sled dog kennel nine kilometers up the road, and because my main form of transportation is a creaky bike with questionable brakes, I don't make it into town too often. I can speak more Finnish to the dogs than I can to people, and when it comes down to it, I'm speaking more to dogs than people right now.

"*Istua, odota,*" I command, setting the dogs' bowls of food on the hard-packed earth. Paws tremble and warm eyes watch me with a degree of devotion I can't shake off. I haven't done anything but stir kibble and expired chicken breast into their tongue-polished tins, nothing more to gain their trust. Still, their eyes latch to mine without fear.

"*Odota,*" I repeat, vowels drawn out, hung in anticipation. *Wait.*

In this wild spread of northern Finland, there are no fences. Boreal forests stretch to lake to bog to timber again, a landscape ambling in every direction without human-staked constraints. The reindeer browsing in the back lot of the grocery store only have one road to cross, then hundreds of unbroken kilometers wherever a compass point spins. The Nordic right to roam guarantees people that same freedom, a law that knocks away private property in the name of mushroom and cloudberry gathering. As long as I don't climb into someone's house, I can amble from riverbank to boat launch without any fear of being somewhere I'm not meant to go.

In the Inari grocery store, I set my armful of items on the register's belt. The clerk scans them, places them in a plastic bag, and mumbles something in Finnish, surely the total stated in green block letters on the screen above the till. I hand her a twenty-euro bill, and she returns my change.

"*Kiitos,*" I say, its spill short enough to hide any accent. *Thank you.* The clerk nods and moves on to the customer behind me without a pause. No one in the store has given me pause. My Swedish heritage passes me as Finnish, and the typical Nordic reserve doesn't ask of much anyway, which feels a lot like home. No one thinks to inquire. I walk through the automatic sliding doors into the low, endless light of summer, where the reindeer know no borders, where the dogs love me for the easiest of gestures.

•

"Hey, bear."

There's no bear nearby that I know of, but it's the potential I'm addressing. The words are habit, a courtesy given to the bear, lips stained with huckleberries, who might not hear me over a mumbling creek. You never want to surprise a bear, especially a grizzly. Like people, her response teeters between fight or flight. She might crash away into the brush, but sometimes she lunges and cuffs with paws meant to rip stumps from earth. I might pass between her and her cubs, and she is, after all, only a mother.

Once, hiking with my dad through a narrow canyon on the south side of the Beartooths, I spotted a minute paw print in the mud of the trail tread, stamp of a bear cub barely longer than my palm. Rather than the curved impression of a black bear, the toes fell in a straight line above the pad. It had rained the night before, and the crisp impression of this small back foot told me that both cub and grizzly sow were somewhere nearby.

"Hey, bear," we called all the way down that bottleneck of canyon, announcing our passage loud over the roar of Sky Top Creek flushed with mist below. We never saw the bears. We followed the trail into lush open meadows, thrilled only by their possibility.

Sometimes I forget to call out "Hey, bear." I get lost in the way the horizon tips into sunrise, or backbones of ridges braiding into a gulch. In lodgepole thickets or coming around a blind corner, the words surface again, a warning wrapped in a smooth, sing-song voice. Sometimes in willow thickets or creek beds matted in brambles, I say, "Hey, moose." Sometimes in springtime, I step softly past mule deer and their speckled newborn fawns. "Hey, mama," I murmur at their sharp hooves.

Mostly I'm heard by nutcrackers, subalpine spruce, arrowleaf balsamroot, voles, bark beetles, yellow columbine, whitetail deer, whitebark pines. Sloping ravines lengthen my throat. Leaves of quaking aspen open my mouth.

"Hey, bear," I say. What I really mean is *I am here.*

•

When I move across the country for grad school, the city sprawls like a grid of concrete boundaries and screeching wheels. I end up buying a bike, eager to know the new landscape through my own energy at a pace to match its scale. I pedal Pittsburgh's neighborhoods into my head—Regent Square, Garfield, the Strip District, Southside

Flats, Edgewood. I follow the rivers, the streets lined with columns of London plane trees, and soon I can pronounce Monongahela without stumbling. Maybe, I think, this physical freedom can chase away the fact that I don't have any mountains to run to.

It works until it doesn't. Until I'm crouched on the floor of my bedroom, knees to chest, unable to get any words out of my throat except a promise to my friend on the other end of the phone. Everything feels hollow.

That evening I force myself out of my room, carrying my bike down the narrow staircase of the apartment building. Some classmates and professors are getting together at a Middle Eastern restaurant in Oakland before a public lecture, and I'm desperate for a feeling of normalcy. The pedals jab into my shins down the final set of steps.

Crossing from Shadyside into Oakland, I miss the green light on Fifth Avenue and roll to a stop in the intersection's center lane. The streets and sidewalks surge with cars and Carnegie Mellon students weary to get home. Low autumn sunlight lifts from building windows and glints off car windshields. I stand in place over my bike, surrounded by the jarring rumble of engines and brakes and horns and bad transmissions. My pedaled freedom of movement is paused, the whole city setting me on edge. In that moment, feet planted on concrete and my bike just an organized collection of metal under me, I've lost any and all movement.

It could have been the street washed in sunlight from too many sources that made me invisible. That's what the driver eventually says—she never saw me. I look up from my handlebars, across the intersection glossed in evening light and blocky shadows from the surrounding buildings, currents of people hurrying across the crosswalk with its signal counting down seconds in red block letters, and suddenly there's a car swallowing the space between us.

My body snaps to paralysis. There's no movement left in me, no way to access it. I open my mouth, but the words don't make it past my lips.

The sedan's impact comes head-on, polished black grille to my front tire, a force that throws me a good half dozen feet back onto the hard surface of the road. I don't remember that airborne moment between collisions—one second I'm standing over my bike, feet planted firmly onto the ground, and then my palms are scraping against asphalt.

The basket zip-tied to the back of my bike snaps off, its contents spread across the street—rain jacket and a handful of books, because I hate going anywhere unprepared. My first and only impulse is to gather these belongings and stuff them back into the cracked basket even before the driver comes out from her car. I know it's just hit me, but it seems an impossible distance away.

"Are you alright?" the driver asks, hovering in front of me like she's afraid to touch me. "I didn't even see you."

A burning sleeve of shame tightens around my throat. Tremors in my jaw pull my lips tight and bloodless. Everyone is watching. Students stop on the sidewalks. Drivers slow on Fifth Avenue. The man in the lane beside us asks if I need him to call 911.

"No," I say, voice choked. "I'm fine, I'm fine." My fingers flutter around the book in my hands. "Was I in the wrong lane?" I ask the woman. "Was I wrong?"

I don't remember her response. I'm not listening for one. I don't remember much of anything except that primal drive to get off the street, to limp away from all those eyes fastened to me, to find my mom, who happens to be in town visiting. I'm a kid again, all independence collapsed into fear.

Desperate for that feeling or normalcy, I still go to the restaurant. "I got hit by a car," I tell my classmates, breathing in and out. My knee and elbow throb. "I'm fine," I add, but there's a stain behind those words. There always is. It's easier to admit the bruises that show, easier to think one impact overthrows another. I don't understand that the pieces are all connected.

I think back to the time my family was out biking together and my brother crashed, breaking his collarbone in two places, how the first thing he did was stand up. I remember the time my first semester of college when I skidded on a patch of ice and bounced my head against the curb, and how that was my first impulse too, to stand up. How I waited in the car while my parents took my brother inside to the emergency room, terrified of those fluorescent hallways. How I knew I'd gotten a concussion from that fall on the ice but never went to the doctor, how the impact triggered a severe bout of depression that a therapist, when I finally made myself book an appointment, told me was just homesickness.

•

The afternoon thunderstorm sneaks up on us, dark clouds hidden behind the cliff bands rising tight above Rock Creek. Thunder claps through the downpour, and by the time my coworker and I get back to our stashed packs, we're soaked through.

On this hitch monitoring campsites in the Absaroka-Beartooth Wilderness, our plan was to move up the trail to a higher lake that night to camp. We huddle under the largest trees we can find, waiting for the storm to move on. I huddle against the trunk of an old ponderosa, and the rain just keeps coming down, relentless, rumbling, frigid.

"Do you think we should just set up camp here?" my coworker asks.

I shake my head and repeat the mantra going through my own head—surely it can't last much longer. We have a long haul up and over Sundance Pass tomorrow, and the higher we get tonight the better. It's my logical response. The deeper reason is rooted in stubbornness. It's only rain, I tell myself, no matter how inclement or sudden or drenching. Exposure to the elements is part of the mountains, part of the job.

The ponderosa isn't doing much good, and I move to a cluster of firs nearby, curling my knees against my chest, pulling together whatever warmth I have left. I press damp fingers into my armpits. I feel sleepy. *I am ice,* I think, and this makes the cold almost bearable, picturing my limbs as hard-packed snow, not muscles and veins emptying their warmth into my core. We just have to wait out the storm, I tell myself. I've been soaked before. My eyes close.

"I really think we should just set up camp here," my coworker says.

I realize I've lost the ability to form an argument, so I nod. The rain is bound to let up any minute, but I still pull myself up and shuffle over to my pack.

Under dripping grand firs I methodically pull out my tent, already dampened as I roll it out across a carpet of fir needles. The shivering starts, first in my breastbone, tugging cords of muscle against my heart. My teeth click together like loose stones. The rain is still going by the time I crawl into my tent, peel off wet clothes, and slip into my sleeping bag. A waterlogged seam on the roof of the tent drips, steady, into a puddle beside my feet.

The storm unpacks thunder and downpour across the canyon and lake for four hours. Gusts of wind loiter and shake the fir branches above me, so that even when the rain finally stops, drops of water scatter across the tent in a taunting patter. I've managed to shiver myself warm again, and huddled in my sleeping bag, a familiar voice of critique warms up too. I'm angry at myself for not keeping a close enough eye on the approaching thunderheads, for overlooking those signs of hypothermia, for toeing that point of no return.

Earlier that afternoon we passed a pile of fresh bear scat off trail near the headwaters of the drainage. We gave up yelling "Hey, bear" over the sounds of our bodies snapping through the underbrush, and I think about where that bear is now. Probably hunkered under a similar copse of firs, but unlike my leaky rain jacket and leaky tent, the bear has a thick coat of blond-tipped fur. When sunlight finally cuts through the banks of steel-gray clouds, he'll shake himself and saunter forward, no possessions on his domed back.

The bear's reality pivots around rainstorms and windstorms and the looming approach of fall. For him, the mountains aren't an escape. They're just home. Exposure is relative, and, cocooned from the rain in a down-stuffed sleeping bag and nylon tent, I'm angry at myself for almost letting that vulnerability kill me, for believing it held all the answers.

•

At the end of our session, the therapist is set on giving me a diagnosis. She rests a yellow legal pad on her knee and taps her pen to the paper. "I like to include clients in this process," she tells me, so they know what clinical name is stamped on their file. This startles me. I see those words as starting points, sharp edges to jump from. Instead, she makes them feel like panels of a box folded up around me.

I try and picture how she sees me. I'm a young woman with knotted hands, stiff in the leather couch. I don't think she notices how I'm holding in my stomach, how my shoulders instinctively hunch to curl around my heart. I don't think she knows that the blue headband holding back my hair is something of a security blanket, a pressured wrap of cloth that keeps me warm on frosted backcountry mornings, that here in the humid city serves a different purpose altogether.

The therapist talks through a few options before settling on general anxiety. "Does that seem right to you?" she asks. "Yours doesn't sound too extreme—no panic attacks or anything."

"Oh, there are those," I say.

"Oh," she echoes.

For a moment, I feel guilty. Her questions were too broad, too open, and I couldn't find any access point to even bring up the catalyst to this appointment. It's always been the issue, struggling to state the obvious. Show versus tell, and I tumble into description.

"Sure, panic attacks," I repeat. Really, I want to tell her where my mind fumbles for comfort in those moments. Iron-streaked stones at twelve thousand feet above sea level, watching and endless, edgeless sky for thunderheads as bright as beargrass. Cream-coated reindeer who slip between clearings without a sound, who watch me with eyes that seem to know why I'm here. Wind-buffeted peaks across the Atlantic where gusts snatch away my voice completely. Lodgepole forests in the dead of winter, snow-muffled silence and the haunt of a mountain lion.

The ring of a crosscut saw through softwood, back and forth, back and forth. Like a breath, a steady heartbeat, a balancing act, until the finely sharpened teeth cut through the dense wood of obstruction.

3

Places to Avoid at Dusk

This place feels like home, but only because there's a guy in flannel eying women from the bar. The music drums something unfamiliar, though that image drags me back—a fizzed spark of gin and tonic at the Rhino on Ryman Street, men wearing flannel for flannel's sake, and women too, and me in the smoky middle, unsure if this was something I wanted, feared, or maybe a little bit of both.

It's early enough in the night that the club bouncer let us in at no charge, but late enough that I'm swaying somewhere between sleepy and tipsy, not sure where another drink will put me. Given the DJ getting set up across the room, I'm figuring the latter. My heart flits under my breastbone, a sensation that's dogged me since adolescence. I dart fingers to my throat, hoping to catch the rumble of blood there, but it's back to a steady drum slugged with wine.

I lift my chin, a trick for confidence I've been trying out, and skirt close to my group of friends. We claim a booth, wander to the bar to order drinks. "A cab," I say, feigning poise, and the bartender doesn't card me. I keep my tab open.

Not that I went out much back home. Weekends I stayed in doing schoolwork while classmates littered old mining quarries with PBR cans. I had a 4.0 to keep up, I told myself, even though half the kids in my AP classes were mooching off their older siblings' IDs. My first dance, senior prom, I wore a strapless navy dress and my grandma's pearls, and I lingered on the pillared edge of the ballroom until a guy asked me if I wanted to dance. I did, but not with him. I scampered back to my group of friends. We left early, shivering in our thin gowns and suits on the walk back to the car. Tiptoed heels across spurs of ice dense as concrete and smooth as glass.

No late nights, no parties, no sliver of recklessness. I set up rules to fill insecurities. My dad taught me which roads to avoid at dusk—Green Meadow Drive, 93 through the Flathead. I didn't know Montana's white crosses were unique to the state until I moved two hours away for college, which was two more hours of worldliness, even if it was the same state. I sipped wine from a bottle passed around a dorm room, pretending it wasn't the first covert drink of my life, that it didn't taste like fear and broken metal. Pretending the warmth in my belly wasn't easing a knot I'd looped too many times to count.

I've tipped back plenty of wine tonight, enough to know that my teeth aren't glinting in the blacklight. Outside of the wooden countertop and lonely-eyed man, not much else reminds me of western bars; the DJ now bobs to hard rap over the dance floor, where neon lights thread through plumes from a fog machine. My group of friends has moved to circle one wall, but I've stayed back in the booth with everyone's stuff. Someone has to watch it, I tell myself. I tell the same to one of my classmates who plops down beside me, returning to her drink.

"I just can't keep up anymore," she sighs. She's one of the older students in our graduate program, retired from the military. "What are you still sitting here for? You should get out there."

"Maybe in a bit," I say. The DJ's beats are too tight and high; I wish there was a heavy thump of bass that would anchor my footfalls to the floor. I wish I could shake out the tightness in my shoulders, a hesitation that's always been there. At twenty-five, I can count on one hand the number times I've been out dancing—though if I work up the courage, tonight might push it onto my left hand.

My head is fuzzed enough from the wine that I haven't bolted to the exit yet, though I'm feeling increasingly prodded that direction by the steadily rising throb of sound. My eyes drift to the dance floor. I have an untiring and unreciprocated crush on a friend, and more often than I should, I catch myself looking in her direction. The decision to come dancing with the group tonight is feeling increasingly rash, especially if all I'm going to do is sit here and pine.

"I used to go out all the time, every base I was at," my classmate says. She traces the joint of her ring finger. "Take my wedding ring off when feeling single, leave it on when I wanted to be left alone."

This tugs my attention away from the fogged-up floor. I tilt my head through the dimness.

"Oh, my husband was gay," she says, sipping her tequila sunrise. "A good friend, also in the military, and this was during Don't Ask Don't Tell. People started asking. So we got married. It worked out great for both of us."

I pull my head back. "That's really admirable of you," I say.

She shrugs. "It was what I could do."

I steal another glance across the room and take a drink. "It still amazes me that wasn't so long ago," I say. "A lot has changed. A lot hasn't."

The music jumps to a patter of sixteenth notes. I'm thinking of the Gay-Straight Alliance club I joined in high school—as an ally, I told myself—and one friend whose parents asked us to pray for him when he came out. Another friend read the message his mom had sent, something about choices and lifestyles and staying on the right path. We all sat squashed together on a row of couches, unsure what we could do except show support. We didn't pray.

The fog machine sighs out another navy-tinted inversion. A couple wearing vests strung in Christmas lights strides in front of our table.

"You're from Montana, right?" my classmate asks.

I nod. "Slower to change there."

She takes another drink. "I had some friends, two girls, who traveled around the country a couple years back. They said of every state, Montana was the least welcoming to them."

The acidic bite of the wine needles up my throat. "Really?" I ask.

My classmate offers a small grimace. "Yeah. They said people were pretty cold towards them once they realized."

"I can see that," I admit, though I won't admit how it still hurts to hear. "There are some good places, some bad. You just have to know which to avoid."

My head trips into a low spin, and I switch to ice water. The music has reached a crescendo too loud to talk over. I'm thinking of Pride parades down Higgins Avenue. The two men beaten outside the Rhino for holding hands.

Dating was like dancing, and I only went to that bar with friends, roaming downtown on Friday nights, swallowing heartburn over a gin and tonic someone got me with a fake ID. I was convinced the flannel-decked crowd saw straight through me. They probably did, in more ways than one.

Here, far on the other side of the Mississippi, I watch eclectic bands of people rolling shoulders and shaking hips through the dim fog, and I'm reminded again that this place isn't home, at least not the home I experienced. It's no wonder most friends from high school scattered across the country before unhinging their closet doors. No wonder I did the same, six hundred sagebrush miles from the Montana state line. I was traveling with a good friend, both of us listless in postcollege doldrums, and an empty, windblown house in southern Oregon seemed as good as a place as any to start telling. Besides that friend, I didn't know a soul there, and that was enough. She convinced me to go dancing a couple nights later. Beneath flashing strobe lights, I wound my fingers around an empty margarita glass. Tilted my hips, swayed my shoulders.

I open my mouth, then close it. My friends and I talk a lot about impostor syndrome, of top-notch writers who still admit to feeling like fakes. Here in this club, I feel contrived, like the wine has blushed a mask to my face. It's slipping away fast. I feel fake among these people who have no hesitations dancing through dusk and dark.

And I feel fake among these memories, lapping back thick with dread, coming-out stories and shocks of violence in a liberal college town. The reality is I go both ways, and for convenience's sake I could fall for a fly-fisherman and sip drinks at the Rhino with no one batting an eye. I did fall for a fisherman once, though never made it past the pining part. At a keg party my junior year of college, I found a spurt of courage beneath all the fear, linked arms with him and spun to pounding bluegrass around the kitchen. Later, as the clocktower across the river counted to midnight, I sped my bike back down Higgins wearing a sober grin. Still pedaling away from that possibility, pedaling hard to a new beat through the cool spring night.

But feelings are never convenient. It took me almost a decade to understand and accept the scope of what I felt, and I stifled my adolescence burying half of those giddy heartbeats out of shame. The other half I weighted with far too much significance, proof against an otherness knotted into a sickness in my gut.

Across the dance floor the friend who I can't shake my feelings for bounces with the beat. I watch a moment too long, enough to knock another chip into my heart. Just friends, she'd told me when I asked. For a second I wish I could snuff out those feelings like I used to.

Plaster a quick, hard wall and turn the other way, let whatever spark that still catches burn a hole of wrongdoing and not one of longing.

I finish my glass of water and tap the ice cubes into my mouth. I swallow one whole. It slips like a pearl down my throat.

I'm not sure why I've shot back all this alcohol tonight, whether against the pining or fear of dancing, but I hate that there's so much looping in my core, that it takes this much to crack my inhibitions. I hate the walls that home stacked, those messages of prayer locked to fault, the silence cutting into kids before they can even ask what it means to feel this way. Montana is a landscape of isolation no matter your gender or orientation. And I'm a product of those limestone gulches, of the people who trim stoicism with drink and break into recklessness like thunderheads over the plains.

Even more I regret the walls I stacked, the rigidity of my own rules that hollowed an absence of experience I can't get back. I'll never get it back. Maybe that's why I'm drunk tonight, chasing a bone-dry thirst to be brash and wild and unburdened by guilt. Maybe I was afraid of alcohol for all those years because I was afraid of what it would dredge up, what a lack of control would loosen my grip on.

And if this was it—watching another woman dance—I wish I hadn't made those rules for myself. I wish I'd gone to bars dim with Marlboro smoke, gone out with anyone, got my heart broken earlier on, learned better coping mechanisms than paralysis and flight. I wish I'd had that covert drink sooner.

I turn back to my classmate. I can still feel the ice water in my belly, how it weaves through the wine's iron slosh, how this sharp contrast reminds me of home.

"I'm queer," I say, which is easier when my mouth is dark with wine, when I'm anywhere but home. Over the music's electronic pulse and shouts of laughter, it's the loudest I've ever said it. There's no room in this dark soundscape for an echo, but still I hear those words thrum and settle to the back of my head.

At the bar, the flannel-clad man has given up his scoping. I'm not going to find any bluegrass tonight; I've got to ease my muscles into this rhythm. It's warm outside, but I know that back home winter just won't quit, that people have given up shoveling snow from their driveways. Soon it'll turn to packed ice, glossed smooth when the overcast retreats to the coast.

"I'm moving back to Montana," I add to my classmate. I think of what she gave up marrying her friend, what he gave up, what they both gained. There are different kinds of protection, I realize, some barriers we don't recognize until the view clears on the other side.

"Who knows how it'll go," I say. I set my glass on the table, leaving a mouthful of cabernet, and stand. "You alright watching our stuff?"

She waves me on. "Absolutely."

Gravity banks below me. I keep to the wall, then merge with my group of friends. They grin, opening the circle wider. I'm not feeling buoyed by inebriation or newfound inspiration, but still, I'm out on the dance floor. The tightness holds fast in my shoulders, muscles rolling up the back of my neck as if hunched under a string of inherited pearls.

It was confusion back then, deep-set denial. I picture my heart like one in cardiac arrest—not stopped, but simply quivering, electronic pulses out of synch. I couldn't tell you what shocked it to a beat I could move to. I couldn't tell you that it doesn't fall back into that shaky baseline every once in a while.

I force my shoulders down, collarbones back. Chin up. I'm not sure what to do with my hands, which always seem to curl into themselves. My self-consciousness has snowballed in front of this one friend—just friends—who moves with a freedom I envy. Her smile sparks in the blacklight.

So I give up caring, leave the regret for the morning, for the lonely hours, for the months ahead when I'm deep in the mountains and find myself, strangely, missing these fast beats and bobbing heads. I remember pedaling my bike through the dark, arms spread wide, a different kind of dance, a different kind of rule broken. Below the fog pools at my feet like rain clearing a valley. I bounce on my toes, churn it from its stalling.

I don't know how to dance. That's a foundation of bass-thudded quarries I never touched, and maybe I'll never reach the underpinning, only know the high ring of its absence. But I can tell you about the roads that catch sunrise while the rest of the world lingers in twilight. I can tell you how to walk on ice, which cracks will hold and which will splinter to midnight waters. I know there's a rhythm like a heartbeat buried in this terrain of sound. I can tell you what love does when coaxed to silence.

4

Siento

I could have killed him, I thought, the way his hand slammed to his chest, fingers splayed, knuckles ridged into white peaks. For a moment, neither of us moved, hung in our separate surprises above the warble of the stream. He hadn't, evidently, heard me coming up the path, feet soft on the packed umber mud. And I hadn't understood the weight of my silence, how it burst before him like a grouse through underbrush.

My voice caught up. "*Perdón*," I managed. "*No sabía. . . .*"

His mouth opened, closed. Red-rimmed eyes fell to the white dog beside him, who'd also jumped, body curled into a comma tapering to a tail between his legs. The dog considered me with sad sable eyes. A pink tongue poked between canines.

"*Perdona, perdóname*." The apologies surfaced faster now, bubbling over the water. "*Yo no quería. . . .*"

I didn't mean to scare you, I wanted to say, but I'd lost the verb, snagged only a noun from the mat of branches above us. *Miedo*. The same fear ebbing from the whites of the man's eyes needled into me, stinging with guilt. *No quería ser visto. I didn't want to be seen.*

A foreign exchange student raised in the high country of Western Montana, I woke at sunrise to skirt the Andalusian heat, ran the backstreets of Granada where shopkeepers soaped the cobblestone and watched me pass. Near the Albaicín, men hung shirts and scarves and jewelry from wooden racks and watched me pass; in Plaza Nueva, they rolled kegs of Heineken from growling trucks and watched me pass. So did the hotel guests breakfasting with *pan con tomate*, the tour guides pulling tricks on Segways in front of the courthouse, the painter adding blossoming peonies to a sketch of the Iglesia de San Gil y Santa Ana.

And I kept running, head down, counting stone slabs until I crossed the Río Darro and could breathe. Here beneath the burnt sienna walls of the Alhambra, watchful eyes dropped away. The terrain rose steeply from the muddy river, crisscrossed by narrow trails and exposed bluffs. Songbirds chattered through thorn-tipped branches; an old donkey bayed in the valley below.

I climbed almost straight up the hillside every morning through Spanish broom and the prickled snatch of rabbit's ear. Kept climbing past hollowed-out caves where young vagabonds sometimes slept, past slick slides of mud that gummed into a cream-colored clay. Then the trails leveled out, ran with the slope and parallel to aqueducts feeding the Moorish palace on the ridge's western tip. Holm oak and pines shaded the intermittent stream, and for a short window during spring, I once watched the water boil with hundreds of spawning frogs. Then watched, distraught, as they worked themselves to death and hung belly-up in stagnant pools.

The packed rise of earth beside the aqueduct could carry me for miles. Sometimes I took it east, deeper into the *dehesa*, farther from the sounds of the city waking up below me, into scrubby oak groves and roosters blessing farmland below. Or I turned west, back towards the Alhambra, and skidded through dense forest mulch beside the rose garden walls. On the other side I could hear people marveling in low voices, snapping pictures of trickling fountains. I caught glimpses of them from certain rises on the trail, but I was out of sight before they had the chance to look back.

I'd seen the man and white dog before, one of the few locals I shared the trails with. He wore a loose polo shirt and faded khakis, walked a steady pace with hiking poles jabbing into the mud. When the weather began to warm, I felt bad for the dog, a shepherd mix, who ambled behind him, panting heavily. This wasn't the first time I'd scared the pair either; descending a dusty set of switchbacks one late morning, I'd spun around a hairpin corner and seen the man shudder, sharply, a dozen yards down the path. Then, it was only a quick "*Perdón*" as I passed, and the dog stretched his dry nose in my direction.

This morning, though, I forgot how quiet I could get. I forgot the minimalist running technique I'd adopted, forefoot first, so that my arches absorbed all impact and sound. I forgot that it had rained the night before, that the water feeding the aqueduct gulped over stones and tree roots. Where the trail crossed the stream, a gnarled copse of vines shuttered out the hot Spanish sun, so that it was difficult to see as well. I'd spotted the man, slender shoulders, gaze locked to the stepping stones over lapping runoff, from a way's down the trail. I forgot to announce my approach, offer a *Buenos días* through the oak and holly.

I forgot, when it came down to it, that I existed. And this is what I was apologizing for—*perdón* and *disculpe* and *discúlpame* and *perdóname* bubbling from my mouth like rainwater. R's rolled into a stutter off my tongue. I'm sorry, I said, for being, for shaking that shawl of observation off my shoulders when I crossed the river below, when my feet left the hard ache of cobblestone. There were too many ways to say sorry in Spanish.

•

My brother and I used to practice being invisible. In the front yard of our childhood home stood a mountain ash with branches prime for climbing. It wasn't impressively tall, maybe twenty feet before the trunk split to twigs, but when we were little, it was enough height to make us feel important. I always climbed higher than my brother, nestled myself into a notch and hummed along with the wind. If our parents came out on the house's front porch, they couldn't see me in this spot, limbs pinched among the branches, eyes a flash behind foliage.

The lowest branch of the ash stuck out like a monkey bar five feet above a carpet of lily of the valley, yellow spurge, and pineapple mint. One day my brother and I came up with a game—hook our knees over the branch and hang upside down, completely limp, fingertips gracing the ground. And we'd stay like that for minutes, waiting for cars to pass on the street. Particularly during long summer days there weren't many, since we lived in a quiet neighborhood with more recent retirees than not. Beat-up Buicks squealed through bad transmissions. Vans swept by to drop off toddlers at the preschool a block away. The mailman, Leon, puttered up to our mailbox and waved.

Still we persisted. We swung dizzy and thick-tongued from the tree in the hopes of a perplexed double-take. But no one bit. We frowned and crumpled, defeated, onto the lily leaves. We reevaluated, upped the ante.

We had to be more extreme. Kids hanging from branches was nothing new, even if we didn't move. So one of us, usually me, climbed up and crouched on one of the lower branches, still in plain view to anyone on the street. My brother, in dramatic flare, sprawled himself across a slab of quartz below the ash, mouth agape. I stretched one arm down towards him, etched false horror on my face. To the passerby it looked like we'd been climbing the tree, and my brother had just fallen and cracked his head on a rock.

It was perfect, we decided. It was hilarious. We could barely keep straight faces. But for the scene, for the reaction, we sobered up, practiced our motionlessness with resolve. This posed more of a challenge; we had to watch both ends of the street for cars, and once we spotted one, scramble to our positions. Remain perfectly still in the hopes that the driver would shoot a lazy glance out the window, resume driving, and then slam on the brakes in shock after putting together what they saw.

The afternoons dragged on. Magpies sparred with crows in the alleyway, a lawn mower droned in the distance, the sun leaned past high noon. A UPS truck rumbled up Sanders Street a block away. The other way, the occasional car hushed down Oaks. Then an SUV appeared at the top of the hill, turned our way.

"Car, car, car," we hissed. We scrambled to the mountain ash, adrenaline drumming in our throats, and assumed our postures. And waited, motionless. My outstretched fingers. My brother's broken-back drape.

The SUV rolled past, not a blink from the driver. So did the next car, an hour later, and the next. Two middle-aged women strolled past with golden retrievers, maintained their gossip without a glance our way.

We were, at first, vexed. But then the absurdity caught on, the realization that as long as we didn't move, we were unseen. We could pose however we wanted. Both of us flopped across the quartz-stone, limp as rag dolls. My brother dangled from a branch, me with villainous eyes above about to pry his fingers from their clasp. We splayed spread-eagle in the overgrown grass holding sticks to our bellies, tragically impaled.

And no one looked, no one beat an eye. This, it turned out, was better than any double-take or rubber-necking—the reaction of no reaction at all. Stillness, we learned, surpassed the context of any scenario. Stop moving in a moving world and you are invisible.

We stilled ourselves beneath the long summer sun. Melded hilarity and violence behind the dam of laughter in our mouths. How easily we could dim our exuberance. How easily we could spring into that tree, or back into the house when our mom called us in for dinner.

•

I read, somewhere on a list of self-improvement tips I took half seriously, to express gratitude in place of regret. Instead of *I'm sorry I'm late*, say *Thank you for your patience*. Spin the focus away from apologizing to acknowledging the other person, the other side of the equation. It's not so much about blame as it is pushing past the urge to assume fault—constantly, repeatedly, endlessly.

I'm sorry for bumping your grocery cart turns to *Thank you for smiling anyway*.

I'm sorry I forgot turns to *Thank you for reminding me*.

I'm sorry for withdrawing turns to *Thank you for giving me space*.

I'm sorry I snapped turns to *Thank you for waiting until I calmed down*.

I'm sorry I'm such a mess turns to *Thank you for listening*.

The impulse runs in the same vein, though. Swallowing fault only gives it grounds to fester inside, hidden and spreading fast. Tossing gratitude into the wind, I've learned, is just another way to go unseen.

•

Once I surprised a fox. By which I mean that once I moved so quietly a wild canine with her pointed nose and ruby-tufted ears didn't hear me. Sometimes I see it as an accomplishment. Other times I'm haunted by that jolt of red fur, how our eyes found each other and she bolted with silent paws into the grass.

Deer watched me in those ponderosa gulches and ridgetops, thick-necked bucks and wary does and spirited yearlings. On the trails threading up from my house, I ran in the company of those eyes—mule deer, turkey vultures, jackrabbits, goshawks, field mice, woodpeckers. Once the brush of a mountain lion's tail through snow, a berry-dense pile of bear scat. A pine martin scampering across fir branches, and red foxes, low lope, always at a distance. Their dens popped up throughout the forest, but they never stayed long, like drifters with earth-blunted nails. My dad hiked the mountains as well, and we kept track of where the foxes were—on the east side of Rodney Ridge, south of Barking Dog Trail, back to the north face of Bompart Hill.

I started running in high school and never stopped. It grew into something of a dependence, the way most people scoop coffee grounds and half slump across the counter as the machine grumbles. Summers when I worked out of a Forest Service office, I was up at five, catching sunrise half an hour later as I spun pine pollen in my wake. In the winter I ran after school, up cold gulches as the sun slunk behind mountains to the south. I abandoned trails, too, leapt over beetle kill snags and limestone guts of old mines. I ran forefoot first, and I was always listening. Jingle of dog tags a quarter mile down the trail. Whir of chainsaws up in a patch of deadwood. Distant crunch of snowshoes as I bounded, unencumbered, through the bright powder.

And I could slip away from the sources of these sounds, from people. I skirted up another trail, or descended a draw on the hidden side of a ridge. I offered smiles and good mornings to other trail users, coughed so not as to scare them if I was coming up behind. "Sorry," I said if they jumped, if the trail was tight, if their dog ran after me, if I sprayed mud or grits of snow from my footfalls. But when I could, I hightailed it in the opposite direction—watching, not watched back.

Below, where the gulches widened to city streets and lodgepoles lost their say to maples, I found only fluorescence-washed classrooms, the seething rapids of adolescence, my brother and I bickering every afternoon as I drove us back from school. Up here sun dogs fractured bluebird skies. Cedar waxwings flocked in dark clouds, dropping like soot onto juniper bushes. Heartbeats swept words from my throat, so that on some mornings hours passed before I spoke. Silence rang in my ears like damp fingers across the rim of a wineglass.

I wouldn't say I was absent. I'd say I was completely present, but present in these immediacies—rain that tasted of orange peels, dark-eyed juncos babbling like the clink of marbles, how to run atop wind-glassed ice without slipping. Whether I was getting out of my head or reorienting it, I was never sure. Call it a daze, call it meditation, call it prayer. Call it escape, call it pursuit. I just ran.

That particular morning the fox was trotting down the trail some fifteen yards ahead of me. This path threaded an easy grade across the mountainside, tread soft with pine and fir needles, ponderosas stretching limbs over dry bunchgrass. When I first saw the fox, I cut my stride and froze in the middle of the trail. I anticipated her knowing eyes catching my movement, sprinting off before I had the sense to remind myself to breathe again.

But she didn't change her pace, and I'd spent enough time under a fox's watch to know she hadn't spotted me either. I exhaled, tested a foot on the quiet duff of the tread. The fox continued down the trail. So I took another step and ran the quietest I've ever run in my life.

Her black-tipped ears perked forward, and I could see the ridges of her shoulder blades rotate beneath fur that rose and fell like a feathered shawl. But the tail didn't move. No sway or bristle or tuck. It floated behind her without regard for gravity or the late summer wind easing vanilla-sweet through the pines. I was wholly enraptured by this contradiction of her tail, how she held it still, even through the bounce of her stride.

Awe edged me too close. Maybe the breeze snagged a reminder of my humanness, or my foot cracked a twig under the dust. The shoulders stopped their rolling, the ears whipped around, and dark eyes glinted with fear. Her mouth broke into incisors and ruby tongue, a nip through the grass. She was gone before I could even stop running.

I'll never forget how she moved without the weight of being seen. What leisure looks like in a wild animal, the most familiar expression I've ever encountered. How, years later, I was running the same trail and heard a rise of yips through the forest, bickering almost, and wondered if this was her litter, if she'd moved back to an old den. I didn't dare step closer. My presence would scatter their comfort, send their proud tails whipping down the gulch.

•

"This city is going to kill me," I tell a friend. "And if I get killed by a car instead of a mountain lion back home, I'll be one pissed-off ghost."

Given, this city has tried to kill me. "Pittsburgh is full of great people," I tell apprehensive family back home. "But once they get behind the wheel, it's a mystery to me where that goes." I know the bright swerve of headlights, drivers behind the windshield lost in some future dilemma. Sometimes they make eye contact as I lunge out of their way, and I want to melt the windows with my glare. Other times I've skirted trauma with no witness. The drivers stare ahead with vacant frowns, throttling to the next light, everything outside those curbs invisible.

I'm right here, I want to scream at them. I want to plant myself on the crosswalk and curse with the screech of their brakes. Pound my palms onto their hoods. *I am a moving body. My bones will break if you don't start watching where the fuck you're going.*

But I don't swear. I almost never swear. Swearing, I learned growing up, means your emotions are out of control. That you are out of control. I coped through internalizing frustration, rotting it to a shapeless sadness, and when that depth swallowed me, I coped through silence. I perfected this magic—stir the saccharine heat in your throat down to the gut, let it condense, and forget how open air makes it froth. Call it melancholy, call it fear. Call it selflessness. But not anger—anger only hurts others, an animal reflex, a bite at close range. Disengage. Pack it deep down, and run off the quiet fumes.

So I don't punch car hoods or add my profanity to blaring horns. Instead I wake up early, a quarter to six, so I can run before traffic gets bad. In summer, this is no problem, but it's late October now, and the sky remains a hazed black. Black when I set out, black through the worst intersections, black down the blocks with sparse street lamps. Gray only creeps into my vision when I reach Schenley Park, a screen of dimness patched by maple leaves sprinkling into the run.

Barely anyone is out at this hour, only the occasional pair with headlamps and reflective vests. I don't care that my running clothes are all dark; if cars don't notice me in broad daylight, I'd rather go totally unseen, even alone in these woods. Some mornings I tell myself I'll bring my headlamp, but I've started getting a high out of running without light. Thrilled something primal in the way I see shapes better out of the corner of my eye.

Appalachian soil moves differently than Rocky Mountain dirt. Less silty, more gummed into bands of clay. These are old stones, worn shale the color of browned butter. They smell of the same unhurried decay as the forest mulch—waxen oak, arterial maple, papery locust. Chipmunks scamper between trunks and hollow logs, all scurry and pip and nut-filled cheeks.

I run the wide path above the stream-split hollow, where only the occasional divot on the tread tests my stride. The canopy, half bare, weaves hardwood branches into a sliver curtain over the run, and I feel like I'm tracing the lip of a cloud forest. I know the terrain rises back up from the stream and onto another path and then paved road, but in these quiet hours, there's no sign of that opposite slope. No sign of earth, even, except the foundation under my careful feet, only woven canopy and that colorless mist, neither dark or light.

When the sky catches a whisper of blue, the crows come out. I hear them gossiping a mile away, throwing insults at the Cathedral of Learning as they flock east. Dozens of them head towards the fine sliver of sunrise. This tradition stays constant every morning, every tail end of night. Some days the crows babble and croak to each other. Some days they fly as a voiceless brush of wings.

I count the weeks, then the days until daylight savings time ends. And when the hours fall back with their heavy traffic, I sprint into visibility, awake with textures I'd forgotten. In Schenley Park, I leave behind the wide, elevated path, dropping into the hollow on the single track that flanks the stream. Before it was too dark, terrain hungry for the crack of my ankles. The trail loops through sandbars and clay-crumbled banks, over and under stone bridges. Chestnuts snap under my feet. Water shushes the sweep of cars above, and I find I don't miss the crows. I could never shake the feeling that the dark pearls of their eyes followed me through this mosaic of autumn, that their rough tongues were talking about me.

Single tracks remind me of the West, of home. Alpine meadows sparked with phlox and glacier lilies. Ponderosa pine savanna, pasqueflower blooming at the first breath of spring. Bear tracks through muddy loam, the thud of a double-bit ax into lodgepole.

This happens when I run too. Distraction, absence. Gone is the damp assurance of an easy winter. I forget the shy whitetail does prancing through the brambles, the raccoons wetting their paws with rainwater. I flirt through past and coax anticipation for the future. Scenarios, empty of even a scrap of plausibility, jump high-strung between the trees.

Today I'm counting the weeks until I go home. I'm thinking of snow, conifers, family, mountain paths that never end but simply braid into game trails, old roadbeds, and granite-bare ridgetops. This park is wild, but it is finite; after a mile, I'll climb out of its relative calm, shift my stride back to concrete and perspective back to distrust. I can see the faces already, smudged behind the windshield, staring at me in limbo at a crosswalk but rarely stopping. Or rolling down a window and tossing catcalls at my bare shoulders, my swinging legs, my body moving because I love to move, because I don't know how else to be, if not to pace existence into my feet every morning, to run with the earth's turn into visibility, morning after morning after morning until I can't remember the last time I woke to sunlight. The objectivity of those stares snuffs out the unbounded rush I keep borrowing from childhood. In those moments I don't want to run and run anymore. I want to bury myself in the dirt, Appalachian or otherwise, and curl my limbs to stillness.

I don't hear the wrinkle of leaves, nor do I see the striped bolt of the chipmunk until it's too late. I'm already midstride, all momentum poised into my left leg. A moment before, only air hung between my foot and the soft earth of the tread. But now there is a body, scampering in terror, and there's nothing I can do.

I roll over him. Trample isn't the right word, nor crush or step on or hit, even. Because I run forefoot first, I feel every bruise of muscle and organ, ribs split like a chestnut husk, whoosh of collapsed lungs. My foot comes down, toe to heel, all the way back, across his belly, plump and round and warm. He would have made it through the winter.

The second my other foot meets muddy earth, I am apologizing. "Oh no no no no," I stammer. "Oh no no. I'm sorry. I'm sorry. I'm sorry."

I am crying, shaking, gasping. Terrified to turn around. But I do, and I watch as the chipmunk convulses in the middle of the path. His pink toes fumble for cover, going nowhere. Whiskers bend into mulch with the thrash of his narrow head.

Of all the West has taught me—how to turn emotion into stoicism, how to smell lightning on the wind—I know the old truth of deer beside the highway, abandoned kittens, mares earthbound with colic. Be it out of compassion or practicality, leave no creature to suffering. Break the doe's neck, put down the kitten, shoot the horse. Spare this seizing chipmunk his final moments of helplessness, wipe the terror from his eyes as he breaks his own back.

My eyes search the woods for something heavy and blunt. It's a different forest now, passive, furtive with its violence, all pliant branches and rotting logs and trees coiled tight around bedrock. The chipmunk shudders towards the closest trunk.

"I'm sorry, I'm sorry," I say to him through my choked throat. I sweep the forest floor again, for anything—a rock, a solid chunk of heartwood. "Why did you have to do that?"

These are the last words he hears. Or sounds, at least, utterance of accusation from my predator's mouth. The body stills. Eyes dim to a scuff of gray.

My hands hang empty at my sides. The stream ripples on, swollen with grainy water.

"Shit," I say.

Right away, I find a firm stick and start carving through the wet forest dirt beside the trail. A runner on the wider path above glances down at me, and I pray she doesn't turn onto the single track. The chipmunk still lies still in the middle of the tread; I don't have the heart yet to explain what happened or tell her to watch her step.

My limbs feel numb as I dig methodically into the earth. Heat pulses into my foot, though, as if the chipmunk's body is still rolling beneath me, and I feel it all again—limber crack of ribcage, pelvis caving in as easy as a spoon to the crust of crème brûlée. Round belly compressed to the ground, all my weight driving into this soft body, this broken body, this quiet body.

I keep digging deeper. If only the chipmunk had waited one second longer before making his dash. If only I'd been paying attention, like I usually do, especially on this trail, where chipmunks have scuttled and squeaked out of my path before. Maybe this one, once. If only I'd seen the warning signs strewn out behind me—flattened squirrels tossed curbside, dead field mice under tumbleweed back home. The bloodshot eyes of the man in Granada, hand clamped to his breastbone, as if trapping his pounding heart, as if desperate to assure himself of its continued drum.

I run because the mountains and forests give me no pause for apology. They've bloodied every given glimpse of my skin, mottled knees and elbows in bruises, frozen fingers and toes, rolled ankles until the tendons went slack. I've been stalked by mountain lions, challenged by whitetail bucks, huffed at by bears, dive-bombed by razor-taloned goshawks. And I keep running because so much of my life is peppered by apologies—my apologies—around every corner, every interaction, every conversation. These places are quiet to me not for their lack of people, but for their lack of a grounded reason to say I'm sorry.

Until this morning. I push the branch into soil, scoop cold dark earth atop cold dark earth. I eye the dead chipmunk again, gauging his size, and return to the hole. It needs to be wider, deeper.

Until this morning I'd forgotten that my presence in the landscape is just that—a presence. That my movements are actions with consequences, and that there is more than just observer and observed. I will scare others. I will hurt others. And those others are not just wild things—deer and foxes and chipmunks—but people too, those close to me as well as strangers behind the grime of windshields. These same people I say sorry to are the same I leave behind when I run, as if absence equates apology, as if either is a sustainable response at all.

My foot continues to ache. I remember that morning above the Río Darro, *perdón* and *perdóname* and *disculpe* spilling from my mouth, and the last words I tried in desperation—*lo siento*. Translated literally, *I feel it*. It's a deeper form of apology in Spain, condolence, compassion, not usually justified to express regret for surprising someone, however abrupt. But I said it anyway. *Lo siento, lo siento*.

And I feel it now, too, everything in the chipmunk's body breaking under mine, everything except his quivering death. For that, I can only give him a damp grave, respite from the sharp-eyed red-tailed hawks that frequent the park. The hole is deep enough, and I stand, carefully drape his banded pelt and perfect paws onto the earth. His mouth is open, and bits of hidden seeds gleam between incisors, crowding there like so many words.

•

I can't get myself to start running in the dark anymore, especially when solstice has passed and the days are discreetly getting longer. I catch predawn dusk, final blink of Venus, and, if the timing's right, sunrise breaking its seam to the east. Starting out in the black night got too wearying. And I'm more careful to watch where I'm going.

Running later in the morning means I meet the growl of school buses in addition to public buses and Mercedes gunning Pittsburgh lefts through intersections. Kids cluster at street corners, usually watched by a pair of parents. I hear their exuberance from blocks away, shouts and shrieks over the constant drone of traffic. Red-faced and giggling, they race up unfenced lawns, swing from the low branches of a crabapple tree.

A crossing guard is posted at Wightman and Forbes, one of the busiest intersections I pass on my way to Schenley Park. The guard is decked out in a full-length fluorescent parka, neon yellow against the gray streets and sky. Each kid gets a warm smile and check-in on how they're doing before she leads them, eyes trained on traffic, across the street.

Sometimes I cross at the same time, going the other direction, buffered by this small chattering crowd. Other times, when I roll out of bed early, it's just me and the crossing guard standing on opposite curbs as buses and cars flash between us. We wait, breaths pluming white in the cold, and then the light changes. I waver, toe the curb. Watch one car tilting into a righthand turn, another behind me creeping into a left across the crosswalk.

The crossing guard steps out onto the street to meet me. She has a worn face creased by an old sadness, I think, or maybe a home after this job that doesn't quite feel like home. There's no distrust in the way she moves, only a calm audacity in the poise of her head. I've watched her stare down a Chevy rattling high on its axels. I've watched her coax conversation from the shyest of kids.

The crossing guard lifts her arms from her sides, opening the span of her visibility. My eyes smart at the fluorescent glare of the coat, the sting of exhaust fumes, the bite of salt on the walk. I start running, meet hesitant eyes with hers as we pass.

"Thank you," I say over the noise of the city, my first words of the morning.

5

Headwater

The river slides southwest without urgency, a slow pane of water held by mud-hemmed banks. I climb over a guardrail and stand on the crumbled lip of a concrete wall as ducks waddle on a spit below. An old arch bridge spans the river to my right, and upriver maples and oaks are blotting colors of fall onto the water's reflection.

The Monongahela. This eastern river is unfamiliar in its wide, muddy drift. I think of the Flathead, the Missouri, the Blackfoot—rivers that move like muscles, rippling and eddying even in the low pull of late summer. In Missoula I often wade into the Clark Fork after running up and back down Mount Sentinel; I know the place where the river stretches across shallow stones and it is possible to stand thigh-deep in the middle of the currents. One winter I walked across snow-scuffed ice to that same center point and lay on my back on the frozen river, feeling, strangely, that this was what it feels like to fly.

At the end of the concrete wall a slim trail cuts down the bank to the muddy spit where the ducks eye me for day-old bread. I could scramble down there to wander across the silty bank, but I feel no draw to the water, no pull to trace my fingers against the flow. I take a swig from my water bottle and step back over the guardrail. I start running back the way I came.

In my first semester of graduate school here in Pittsburgh, I've found sloped green parks thick with humidity in late summer, brown and bare in early winter. I share hidden single tracks with whitetail deer and mountain bikers who've built ramps into steep draws. The land here is round—canopies rolling like the heads of cumulonimbus clouds, old hills rising and dipping down to the rivers. I'm used to a pointed landscape of sharp granite peaks and evergreen needles, but the spread of autumnal colors in this city still tugs an ache of awe in my throat.

My run down to the Monongahela ends up totaling ten miles round trip, and I spend the rest of the day drinking black tea against a creeping exhaustion. I pop another multivitamin into my mouth, but already I feel that familiar hollowness in my limbs, my blood slack like the river's flow. I've fought iron-deficiency anemia for years, and I should have known better than to push this morning's run as far. I'm missing Montana. I'm missing home. My legs itched for distance, and I just kept running.

That evening one of my roommates cooks a pot of chicken hearts and gizzards, well seasoned in curry and pepper. At the grocery store, she tells me, she had to ask for them, and a butcher pulled the package from a back freezer. Back home in Nigeria, she adds, they're considered the best parts of the bird, and the most expensive. Resting in a Styrofoam tray on the counter, the hearts and gizzards are a heavy crimson, and sizzling in oil and spices they waft a dense metallic smell throughout the apartment.

Hearts and gizzards oppose soft white breast meat; they're the muscles invaluable for the bird's survival. Her gizzard, a rough pouch full of gravel, grinds down grain and insects and whatever else she eats, and her heart pumps blood until the final moment of slaughter. Each organ gleams scarlet with blood caught in knots of muscle, and I know, today especially, I should feel a deep craving for iron-rich meat. That morning's run has sapped iron from my bloodstream, where it's needed to haul molecules of oxygen throughout my body. This is one of the first prescriptions against iron-deficiency anemia—eat more meat, red meat in particular. But I don't. The smell of the hearts and gizzards sticks like slag against the back of my throat.

•

One early winter in college, I went with a group of fellow University of Montana students to an organic farm northeast of Great Falls. It was the weekend before Thanksgiving, and we were there to help slaughter turkeys. Five dozen hens with umber plumage warbled in a dim and dusty barn. Our group split into different jobs involved in processing a live turkey into the carcass wrapped tight in white plastic, and I ended up a catcher, at the head of the process. The hens flapped their wide wings and darted across the barn's straw-strewn floor as I chased them with a neighbor's eager son. In the beginning, with fifty birds crowding the space, we could easily snatch a hen. I would gently press my hand into the turkey's back to hold her down, then stretch my arms around her wings and soft breast. The minute her wings were pinned to her side, she quieted. Black marble eyes watched me as I held her by the barn door, my heart rushing like a shallow river.

Outside the barn was the slaughter shed, where four or five metal cones hung nailed into wood boards. Below the cones, which had open tips, five-gallon buckets rested among straw and yellow grass. I brought the hen next to the cone, and with the help of a classmate we tipped the turkey headfirst into the cold metal constraint. Her head poked out the bottom, beak ajar and eyes swerving with the tip of gravity. With my right hand I held her feet against the soft down of her underside. Her rough legs were dense as branches of mountain ash.

I can still feel the grate of the sharp knife across her wrinkled neck. Colors stick in my mind too—cardinal-red blood spilling from the jugular hot and slick into the bucket below, where it settled dark like red wine. Buckets of blood gleaming in the sun. Splatters of blood across my boots and coat. Smears of blood settled into the creases of my palm, a death stained on my hands.

Wind rolling in from the plains tussled bits of hay and tufts of down feathers around us. On breaks I stared out across the fields threading into sharp-edged plateaus. These were free-range turkeys, I told myself. They rummaged through stalks of pasture grasses after grasshoppers and ants, flocked to lines of heritage barley come wintertime. Around them was the comforting spread of prairie and quilted farmland. Freezeout Lake lay a dozen miles to the west. I imagined the turkeys' crinkled heads turned upward in the spring, and thought perhaps one or two would offer a high gobble to the waves of snow geese arcing across pale blue sky. I told myself that was something, the bright air and pursuit of grasshoppers.

But I didn't eat meat that Thanksgiving. Bumping elbows with uncles, aunts, and cousins at my grandparents' farm in the Flathead Valley, I stared at the dark thigh meat traced by strings of veins, the oily intercondylar fossa where a whole leg had once been. I passed the hefty porcelain platter along to my grandpa. Not because the experience of slaughter had turned me vegetarian, but because I didn't know where the turkey came from. I guessed enough—a stagnant, dim shed packed with hundreds of white birds who had never seen open sky. Pumped with antibiotics, limping on twisted legs. I didn't know how they were killed, but surely not with human hands. Surely not beneath the same sky of their hatching and roosting and foraging.

•

I pull a bag of salad greens from the fridge's crisper drawer. I know I should at least be eating some form of protein, but that craving is clouted away by the smell of the chicken hearts and gizzards. I microwave a bowl of peas, scrub the fine roots off two carrots, and dump a generous dusting of parmesan cheese on my salad. My roommate smirks at me. It's the chalky, cheap kind, but there's something about the starchy texture that I can't get enough of.

Looking up iron-deficiency anemia online, I once found that this craving falls in line with other common symptoms. Among the weariness and dizziness, the cold hands and feet, the restless legs, people low on iron in their blood also develop a desire to consume substances with little nutritional worth. Namely, the Mayo Clinic told me, starch, dirt, and ice. *Ice*, I thought, pulling the pieces together. In high school I used to freeze a Nalgene water bottle every night, and come afternoon the melting process would leave a crisp blade of ice inside, which I cracked with an insatiable hunger between numbed teeth. That, coupled with my shaking the bottle to break apart larger chunks, drove some friends and one English teacher nearly mad.

Snow, too, though the Mayo Clinic doesn't mention that. On my winter runs in Montana I cultivated a nuanced taste for snow, pinned to qualities of texture and moisture. Soft brushes of freshly fallen flakes lingering on my face. Gritty grains of sub-zero snow, or wide crystals of a thawing crust. In the South Hills of Helena I tasted a powder bright as needles of young ponderosa pines, while the damper climate of Missoula infused snow with the citric tinge of Douglas firs. In the Mission Mountains snow rests heavy beneath boughs of grand firs and redcedars. My grandpa would take me riding deep into those dark copses, where grizzlies left curled blond hairs in splinters of snags. We followed old logging roads, and even in July and August snowbanks clung to shadowed bends in the path.

My mouth waters with the thought of snow, and I compensate with a bite of iceberg lettuce. The crisp, watery stalk, I realize, is almost equally non-nutritious. Mid-November in Pittsburgh means the deciduous forest has almost finished dropping its vibrant canopy, but back in Montana I know snow has already settled in the high country. Ice creeps back across alpine lakes of the Rattlesnake north of Missoula. In the Beartooths avalanches have already scraped down from high plateaus. Across the Helena Valley I can picture the low yellow pastures of the Sleeping Giant blanketed in snow. My mom used tell my brother and me that, anticipating winter, the giant had brought out a warm white sheet to cover his legs.

I retreat from the smell of rich meat, settling in my room with the parmesan-powdered salad. My roommate is a fantastic cook, and usually I can hardly stray from the aromas she conjures in the kitchen—curried rice dishes, vegetable and okra soups, chicken simmering in white wine vinegar, German chocolate cake draped in a coconut frosting. "What're you making?" I regularly ask after coming back from class, and feel that rural accent slipping through: *Whatcha makin'?* Something about being in the East has coaxed that subtle drawl from my voice, a way of speaking I'd previously only ever picked up while working in the backcountry or after a couple hours at my grandparents' farm. The *t* evaporates from my *winter*. I figure a lot more than I think.

But *creek* rarely tumbles to *crick*. It would take hours of conversations with my grandpa about horses and splitting logs before the possibility of *ennit* would enter my mind. For much of my childhood summers, I wandered carefree through the streams and pastures of my grandparents' farm, relishing in a pace of life that had everything to do with the turn of sunlight and afternoon thunderstorms. My grandpa raised a herd of black Angus cattle, and every morning I jumped into the cab of his red Ford flatbed, our horses saddled and waiting in the trailer, to go check the cows with him. He drove slow down the county road, windows down and a mug of coffee steaming beside the gear stick. I don't recall the coffee spilling much, if any. My grandpa had to look at fences, and the flow of irrigation ditches, and the pivot of sprinklers in potato fields.

He was always observing. One summer he watched black bears browse on wrinkled fruits of serviceberry trees. "Want one?" he asked me after we'd halted our horses by the brushy tree, and I tentatively chewed through the meager, mealy fruit and gravel-like seeds. "They don't taste like much," my grandpa admitted, but he pulled another handful from the thorny branch. Later, my grandma looked the berries up and found that they were rich in antioxidants, on high demand in health food stores. My grandpa shrugged. "The bears were eating 'em, so I figured they must be good," he said.

With the exception of riding and trips into town, I abandoned shoes at the farm. Barefoot in the creek, chasing guppies, leaping away from gardener snakes. Barefoot in the hay field and the yard, even after twice stepping on black jacket wasps. Barefoot across manure and buttonweed in the corral, walking among the horses when they came in to drink from the water trough. I blew softly on their velvet muzzles, and on their warm breaths I smelled dry grass, alfalfa, corn stalks my grandma pitched over the fence from the garden. I smelled carrots and bruised apples she would send out to the barn with me, plucked by rough lips from my palm. Nose to nose, this is the way horses greet each other. An exhalation speaks of what you've eaten, which is no different from where you've been. And where you've come from forms who you are.

My favorite unshod place was the garden, where rich moist earth curled soft between my toes. I meandered among rows of sun-split tomatoes and thigh-thick zucchinis, the high hedge of corn and ruffled lane of lettuce. Afternoons I snacked on snap peas, raspberries, green beans, carrots. I rarely scrubbed black soil from the carrots. I crunched into sweet roots and rich earth just the same.

I finish my meager salad and scrape up the last of the parmesan with my fork. There's some nameless craving edging my stomach, but I can't place it well enough to muster another trip to the kitchen. I'm remembering my grandma's cooking, the simmer of chicken noodle soup on the stove, her Thanksgiving pies made from pumpkins chilled in the dim food cellar under the house, where feral cats slunk among crates of onions and squash dusted in fine earth. There were meals where everything on the table, with the exception of the bread and butter, came from the farm. Steaming potatoes that flaked crisp like mica. Bright emerald asparagus from the bushy rows behind the tomatoes. Glossy ears of corn with kernels that burst sweet as honey. A beef roast from one of last year's cows, a cow born in the pasture above the house, slaughtered there in the valley. A cow I watched nudge through rain-softened Johnson grass and bed down among snowberry brush when the sun fell too warm on her dark flank.

Cravings. The body knows what it needs, what it pines for. Sitting in my Pittsburgh apartment, limbs heavy and stomach twisting, I know this is a hunger I cannot fill, a comfort I cannot consume. I can take vitamins that stain my pee fluorescent yellow. I can force a burger once in a while, brighten my diet with leafy green vegetables. I can fall in love with an eastern fall, with golden maples and bickering blue jays. But I cannot run this thirst away, nor drown it in exhaustion. There are supplements, and then there are sources.

•

Once I sat on the bank of the Middle Fork of the Flathead River in a soft gray dusk. I was with the same group of college classmates I would later slaughter turkeys with, and we were nine days into a backpacking traverse of the Bob Marshall Wilderness Complex. No pack train, no resupply, only the power of our aching feet. The river swept past like a deep blue vein. Earlier in the afternoon, I had ambled barefoot across the sandbars, climbing over driftwood and cooling my legs in the strong rush of snowmelt. Beneath a polished old stump, I found a string of paw prints in the sand. Coyote, I guessed, adding the mark of my own bare feet beside them.

In the cool fall of evening, we passed around a large cut of riverbank one of our field instructors had found a few miles downstream. The dense mass of earth was a slick, gritty clay the color of storm clouds swallowing a mountain. I kneaded a ball in my palm and held it to my face. It smelled of rain and old stone worn from lightning-streaked peaks. Sharp as pine and fir needles. Broad as the first drape of snow. Smooth like the river's weave, an urge pulled south to softer earth.

Tacked into the walls of my room are a patchwork of maps and posters, most of places in Montana. I stare at the flat panes of paper, at the green shades of relief and tight topographic lines. Mountains—that's what I tell people I miss most out here. Deep snow and quiet and bright open sky. But I've forgotten the lines opposite ridges, the cuts of creeks and rivers branching like arteries below. Rippled muscles full of grinding stones. A fluid tongue carving into root-held banks. I've forgotten the alluvium glinting fool's gold or seeping left-over metals behind old dams. I've forgotten how I follow these bodies upriver, where snowmelt drips steady from fields starred by glacier lilies, where stone calves to sediment.

On the bank of the Middle Fork of the Flathead River, I stared at the clay slip of riverbank curled into my palm. Something as old as the river and fir-brushed mountains tugged at my gut. It had little to do with the scarcity of iron in my blood. It had everything to do with cutthroat trout swirling in cobalt pools, with the calligraphy of canine prints across willow-clutched sandbars. I opened my mouth and touched my tongue to the silken earth once, twice. It tasted deep, and dark, and quiet.

6

Stories That Hold Water

The young woman liked to think of herself as a westerner. She was born in Colorado, after all, always felt cradled by the Rockies, has spent most of her life in Montana. She's rambled down to northern Utah a couple times, woven in and out of Wyoming where the only marker of the state line was gnawed down by marmots, taken a liking to both the high desert and achingly green sides of the Northwest. She can ride horses and drive stick and sharpen an ax by hand, as if those are qualifiers. She collects maps, mug handles from ghost towns, old halters, stories, feathers left on backcountry trails.

One summer, her boss, who was born out east in Pittsburgh but has lived in Western Montana for some time, tells her a story. They are en route to climb the highest peak in the Rattlesnake Wilderness, and, still hours before full sunrise, she doesn't catch the trickster's gleam in his eyes. Her imagination stretches into the details, a dog to an open green field.

•

Once, the story goes, there was an old-time packer who strung his mules through the Bob, guiding big-name clients who payed big money to tag along. He was something of a celebrity throughout Montana and some of Idaho, could tap a mare's hock and she'd pick up her foot without a fuss. Every summer he loaded up his team, hauled them north to the blue-stacked horizon. Sometimes he rode with other quiet men with loud laughs, other times with wide-eyed travelers. The packer understood. You couldn't walk or ride through this place without wide eyes, even if you'd stuck out a dozen winters.

It was a lot to carry into the backcountry, tack and feed for the stock, and feed for the riders—all that good elk steak, flapjack flour, potatoes for fries. These weren't A-frame tarp sorts of trips. His clients could strut their fringed chaps inside the tents; maybe they brought a small wood stove to burn away the morning's chill.

The old packer brought ketchup for the bratwursts, but damn those glass bottles, heavy and one clink away from turning to crystalware teeth against his mules' hides. So he found a squeeze bottle, a decent cap, rigged up a solution that spared the thump of palm to glass.

One trip the packer showed off the Bob to some easterners named Heinz. Listening to this story, the young woman pictures them trekking through the Great Bear like she did once on foot. Maybe the packer pastured the stock at Schafer Meadows, on the other side of the fence from an airstrip weaseled into the wilderness. Small-engine planes buzzed in, bounced their tires on mowed turf. The old packer scowled. He pitched camp closer to the river, enough that the current muffled those whirring machines.

Morning brought mist trailing an empty airstrip, cold-nipped silence and horses sighing from the trees. Coffee dripped and steamed in the wall tent. On a foldout table, fork-fluffed eggs and sausages from last fall's elk hunt and home fries cracked with pepper. The packer set out slabs of butter, cups for the coffee, ketchup held in a plastic sleeve.

The Heinz boys loaded up their plates. Riding makes you hungry, they were right about that. One swore he heard a grizzly huffing around his cot early in the morning, spooked him off with just the click of a pistol's hammer. He stopped midtale reaching for the ketchup. Fingers hovered midhold. Eyes locked with his brother's. A squeeze bottle, their ketchup. His hand curled around the bottle and the ketchup shot out across his home fries. The other brother took a turn, eyes wide and sparking. Both bothers gaped and grinned. They passed the bottle between them, back and forth, laughing and slapping Carhartt thighs. The old packer stayed humble, smirking beneath his mustache. Can't show emotion to these folks, can't let them on to this old and easy secret.

They rode and ate well the rest of the trip. Even when a sun-sleepy owl spooked the pack train, the old packer puffed out his chest, proud when the line straightened out, proud when the clients fell wordless before the sunset like marble on fire. Maybe they followed the Middle

Fork all the way to Highway 2, or hopped the Divide and came out along the Teton River. The route itself isn't of much importance. Either way was beautiful. Either way was a long and welcome view.

But when the trip was done, those Heinz boys turned their shoulders away from the mountains, heading back east to Pittsburgh, where soot stained the sky and the stone pinnacles of buildings. They returned to the indoors world—oil-hungry office chairs and scribbles on legal pads and stair-steps of numbers and figures. They pictured their name haloed in red, *Heinz Heinz Heinz* down grocery aisle after grocery aisle. They thought of this motion, snatched from a river valley deep in the Rockies. Not a shake and splatter, but a squeeze, a clasp, a grip and release.

Maybe they did give the old packer credit where credit was due. You never know. But most likely it didn't bother him much. He'd already earned fame in his packing skills, hands soft with stock, knowledge of the routes and river valleys splitting through the Bob. Forget innovation in board meetings, family legacy, consumer demands. Take blue skies, take rough trail. Take a packer who loads his mules perfectly balanced on either side.

•

You can lead a westerner across the Mississippi, but, well, you know the rest.

For two years the young woman was always thirsty. She'd been working and traveling out West, dodging a strange feeling that the mountains and dry air and land-tied people all felt stagnant to her. It was like trying to remember the color of the house you grew up in.

She moved out east for grad school to shake things up, but she found Pittsburgh too locked in suburbs and small sky. She felt drenched—drowning, sometimes—no matter the gray, dry rattle of winter. She continued to wear a hat pricked with feathers on one side, hated how she stood out but also how she didn't know herself without it. The rolling hills of the city bucked her sense of direction except to pull it back west, pointing over the Mississippi like the confluence of the Allegheny and Monongahela Rivers. To ease the transition, the young woman told herself all sorts of stories. Many weren't true, which just made her hold on tighter.

She did make connections. First a friendship with another young woman from Utah, both of them caught in the school gym during a thunderstorm that blinked the electricity out. Against advice from campus security otherwise, they both bolted into the downpour, gleeful in the danger of it all.

She wrangled friendships with people from that round-mountain side of the continent, Ohio and New Jersey and Alabama and Pittsburgh itself. But the connections built slowly. The young woman hid in the dim city parks before sunrise, behind the excuse of western stoicism, among stories of bears and riding bareback and swimming in alpine lakes. Most afternoons she holed up on the second story of the library, the quiet study floor. She grew tired of explaining what a snag was, heard the ping of her Minnesota- and Canada-tinted accent when she pronounced the word.

Once, even farther west than home, she had started to fall for a woman singing John Prine's "Angel from Montgomery" in a crowded bar brushed all around by sagebrush. She was working for the singer's family on a ranch perked green by flood irrigation, learning to stock dams in the ditch so snowmelt from the mountains pooled blue and cool across the fields. It was such a ridiculously cliché thing to do, sit in a brewery and feel her belly warm with something more than her drink, but when it comes down to it, the young woman has never had much say on who or what she falls for.

All her time in Pittsburgh, she thought of the song. She sang it, often badly, in the shower, still scrubbing Montana dirt from her skin. She pretended that she wasn't in an apartment building with other units sharing the echo-prone walls, that some mornings she didn't hear the upstairs neighbors singing too.

The feelings attached to those words had gone by then, dispersed like sawdust in a breeze, but the young woman kept hearing an echo of that line—*Just give me one thing that I can hold on to, to believe in this living is just a hard way to go*. Not that her living was so hard. She just had a habit of letting everything weigh on her all at once, a pelleted rush of downpour. The young woman thought she knew home, thought moving away wouldn't hurt so deep.

In Pittsburgh she took to keeping a scrap of paper listing things that she could hold on to—just one thing, line by line, like an inventory of food items to shove into a pack. Some were words spoken, bursts of kindness, a risk she took that did or didn't pay off. Some were stories wrapped in pride. Some were stories she's still finding the guts to finish. Some were stories she's still finding the guts to start.

The high stone buildings, by then, were long scrubbed clean of their soot. The young woman paced late afternoons to the street ends, cutting down a block and turning back to walk the other way. She ran and ran, just about the same loop every morning to a pond that muted the city sounds. One year a flock of Canada geese wintered there, and come spring she watched with longing in her throat as they trumpeted their way north.

Sometimes she wandered across the river, along the railroad tracks, looked up at high red brick buildings emblazoned *Heinz*. Once she followed a trio of turkey vultures—took a couple lefts beneath and atop bridges, trailed the warble of Nine Mile Run, and found herself under a bright chunk of sky and eye to eye with a brighter river. Later her maps told her this was Duck Hollow, the smooth Monongahela easing past like glass, the Homestead Grays Bridge spanning its silver-beamed reflection just downriver.

How she wanted to belong to that place, just a little. None of this Wild West nonsense, checkerboard land claims, acres and acres stolen and titled to a single name. Maybe not even like the old-time packer to the Bob or the Heinz family to Sharpsburg, both still wrapped in a semblance of that theft. She wouldn't realize she'd been strutting her out-of-place-ness in a desperation that someone would take it from her, strip her of the weights bound to shatter against her back. Hold it up to her like a skinned hide, show her how ridiculously cliché it was too.

At its highest vistas she loved that place, and down in the mulched gullies she hated that place. Which, when it comes down to it, means she knew it better than she thought, and that she knew herself less. She paced and paced. The second winter was colder, more like home, and the quiet pond froze solid. One morning the young woman edged off the lip of its shoreline and found that the ice could hold her. She skidded and whirled through a soft down of snow, skimming fingertips across cracks that spurred deep into the cold blue.

•

Here's another story the young woman stumbled across, still searching for connections, still stretching details so she could fit her narrative in between the fissures. It's one that the Heinz name, decades down the family line from just ketchup, has tried to help dredge up into truth.

This was back in the days of the Cold War, just a couple years before Minuteman nuclear silos started popping up on the Great Plains of Montana. One frigid January day, Pittsburgh stuck in its usual gloomy gray, a B-25 military bomber was completing a training run from Reno to Harrisburg. Banking over the triangle point of Pittsburgh, the bomber spluttered out of fuel. It turned towards the Greater Pittsburgh Airport, which turned out to be too far away, then back towards the Allegheny County Airport. That possibility was too far as well.

The major onboard made the call to steer into the Monongahela River, speckled with ice and greased in oil slicks from the slag dumps. He stared at the slate body below, set his teeth until his jaw pulsed. This would be the place. The river lapped over flat brown brush and sandbars pocked with garbage. The Homestead High Level Bridge, today's Homestead Grays Bridge, looped its reflection over chips of ice. The major squinted again at the wide pane of water, thinking about depth and impact, or maybe thinking of nothing beyond the rattle of his hands, fingers squeezed bloodless-white into palms.

The engines quit over West Homestead. Picture that silence, a machine forged to haul explosions of sound, thousands of pounds of airborne thrust gutted of its power. Snuffed to the whistle of cold wind and anticipation heavy as glass.

The bomber's wheels, pumped for the hard grasp of asphalt, skimmed and collapsed into dark water. Next came the plane's body, a wall of foamed white spraying towards the bridge. Great rushes of air burst from the cabin and cargo bay, and so did the crew, six men crawling from the plane as it dipped, inch by inch, deeper into the river.

Only four made it out. The young woman can't find much on the logistics of the men's drowning, and she doesn't want to put herself too far in that moment. All she knows is that two men made a break for the vine-knotted shoreline while the others waited with the sinking bomber, clinging to the ice-lapped metal. And those two men, the captain and staff sergeant, slipped with numbed limbs into the black water. No one found the bodies for months.

Hours after the ditching a cutter vessel from the Coast Guard managed to slip a cable around one wing of the submerged bomber. Tables of ice shushed past, and the ship dug its anchor into the river's muddy floor. For a moment, all the lines held. Then the cable snapped, or a knot worked itself free, and the plane's wing breached into gray air one last time before foundering away.

And it foundered into conjecture. Some murmured about UFOs. Some speculated there was nuclear cargo onboard, or Las Vegas showgirls shuttled to entertain the men weary or bored from a quiet war. Pittsburgh's buildings stood coal dark, watching, and the Mon oozed with remnants of coke and smelt. Maybe, many thought, the polluted river simply ate away the bomber, propeller by propeller, wing by wing.

Aided by the Heinz Historic Foundation, the B-25 Recovery Group formed with the goal of finding its namesake remnants. They held meetings and jotted down notes and figures on legal pads. It must have sunk into an old gravel pit, they decided. The group sent divers and remote-control devices to putter through the murk. Over and over they came up empty. If it hadn't yet gnawed the aluminum away, the Mon's silt was still obscuring whatever waited down there.

So the recovery group tried side-scan sonar, tugging a sensor above the riverbed, back and forth, back and forth. Bursts of noise shot out in conical waves, and those on the surface listened intently for the shorter ring of an echo. The terrain of the river bottom slowly unfurled—dips and ridges and shelves and soft crevices of mud. Old channels and new ones, scars cut in from the rain-deep hollows above. Waterlogged oaks that weighed as much as a plane engine, but no plane itself, not a single strip of metal.

The group and Heinz Foundation doubled down. They filed permits with the EPA and Army Corps of Engineers. Every year their calendars flipped past the day of ditching, the thirty-first of January, on to February. Maybe not the aluminum shell, but something must be left. Just one thing. The Monongahela only flowed twenty feet deep, the gravel pit just a little more at thirty-two. When it came down to it, there was nowhere for a plane to go.

After two years, when the young woman moves back west, she can't get enough ketchup. She can't really explain it, just that she has a craving for Heinz about every night there's a roof over her head.

Her days sometimes feel like a chipped record, routines rounded into the same motions that tone her shoulders strong. She lives in Missoula now, on Missoula Avenue, in the Rattlesnake neighborhood. She works in the Rattlesnake National Recreation Area and the Rattlesnake Wilderness, and every day, in one way or another, she touches the waters of Rattlesnake Creek. Mornings she drinks and drinks those waters until she's peeing every twenty minutes. She had this habit in Pittsburgh, too, in and out of coffee shop restrooms, up and down the library stairs. Evenings she dunks herself in the high lakes and lets the underwater silence fill her ears until her forearms go numb. When she returns to the world of birdsong, her legs wobble against solid ground.

The Rattlesnake is hardly a smudge compared to the heft of the Bob. Still it's a wildness that fits her. Out there luxury is a two-person tent and cocoa powder shaken with brown sugar. She carries in her own gear, and the weight of her pack sometimes gnaws sores onto her hipbones. When she lets the pack thud to the ground, she feels like she could just float up beside the slim shoulders of spruce and fir.

This is it, the young woman tells herself every sunburst of morning, even when the light is clotted with rain. No stake of ownership, just this blue stack of mountains to the north, one quiet and beautiful thing that she can hold on to.

Her grandma gives her potatoes from the farm at the base of the Missions, fat on Flathead water, and carrots ringed in dark earth. The young woman plucks herbs from her own backyard—sage, thyme, oregano, chives that she waters every other night as Mount Jumbo shines gold above. Come winter elk will drop south out of the Rattlesnake, zigzag the mountain's snow-smooth face like lines on white paper.

She sips a glass of red wine and chops the vegetables. She listens to the news, or talks with her roommates, or lets her imagination lope away from the slick potato cubes. She throws all that food in a pan—the russets, the sweet carrots, the herbs, spears of zucchini and chops of broccoli, enough garlic to keep the ticks and mosquitoes at bay when she's sawing trees for work. She drizzles some olive oil over top and sparks everything with salt. Sautés it together, no compass-bound culture here, just a chronic hunger that, when it comes down to it, isn't just about food.

The young woman thinks a lot about those two years. Stumbles and downright pitches into mud and a depth of homesickness that was never really about home. She doesn't necessarily miss Pittsburgh as a place, but as a rough-cobbled lump of time, something she knows she'll never get back. She's alright with that. She has the friendships, hours-long conversations in parked cars as locust leaves dappled the night. Flooded rivers and dance parties in the kitchen and enough laughter to crease new lines onto her young face. She has the taste of its water in her mouth.

In the cradle of Rattlesnake Creek, she scoops her dinner from the pan and holds the squeeze bottle in her callused palms. And she squirts ketchup overtop, back and forth, back and forth. It's always Heinz. Working down her grocery list at the store, the young woman won't settle for anything else. She traces the vinegar-sharp condiment like elk tracks across Jumbo, like the trail up the Bob's Switchback Pass, like the hollows ruffling through oak and sumac down the Monongahela.

She spoons out the rest of the vegetables, layering the crimson among what good Montana dirt can grow. Then she squeezes out a little more ketchup. Alright, maybe more than a little more. She goes outside to eat, where the air is dry, where the horizon is spiked in pine, where the sky unfolds high and comforting above her.

•

Here's a trick, one the young woman learned from the owls. They're all about noise, echoes, skulls tipped asymmetrical to catch the bounce of sound. The bones of the dished face look like a mistake, pinched high on one side, slumped low on the other. The irregularity improves their hearing, widening the frequency of noises they can pick up. A rubber boa sliding across tamarack needles. A kangaroo mouse tiptoeing through paper-dry bunchgrass.

But owls are also about sight. Take a look at those wide, bright eyes. They're actually held tight into the eye sockets, no room to budge for a quick side glance. The owl moves her head up and down, back and forth, up and down, back and forth. She changes her perspective for a better understanding of what's in front of her. Tackle the unknown at another angle and it's not quite so daunting.

The young woman takes this trick into basins thick with fir and spruce. Searching for a lake, the sway of her head back and forth splits the canopy into two distinguishable walls—whatever is straight ahead, and whatever stands behind the gap over open water. There. There is the cool blue body she's looking for.

Or she extends the practice across the slope, zigzags her way over terrain where there is no trail. Back and forth between ridges and spongy meadows, buttes the color of apple peels, unnamed streams warbling fast. Scree slopes where pika chirp and scamper, hillsides blotted with beargrass, geraniums, huckleberries. Snowfields ready to skid her into cut-up knees and bruised elbows. Horizons steep enough that she watches the sun set three times as she rounds the slope.

For all her backs and forth, all her squinting through lichen and pine boughs, the young woman rarely gets lost. You wouldn't believe it, the way she trips and cracks ankles and weeps at the empty miles. It's just that sometimes she's got to go too far west, too far east, double the distance before she can figure out the best way to trudge between the two.

•

For two autumns, two winters, one summer, and two springs, the young woman laced up her shoes and ran down to the Homestead Grays Bridge a couple times a month. Sometimes there were fishermen casting off from the concrete wall, campfire remnants, birders wearing binoculars like medals. Snapping turtles puttered through the muddy shore, and geese couples bickered with mallard ducks on the banks. Gulls looped over the spot where, sixty years before, a bomber on a training run had ditched into January-gray waters.

It's the full truth, no trickster's gleam or wild speculation. The young woman didn't know that place's history, had no way of seeing that the river bottom lapped a little deeper under the currents, had no way of hearing engines echo as quiet as bird's wings. All she knew was the long spur of shoreline tangled in flat brown brush and pocked with garbage. She knew the wide swell of the river lifted the horizon above her, that every time she visited she fell a little for both water and sky.

When the second summer crept near and the young woman steered towards home, she could bear leaving the land. It was the goodbyes to people that tugged her heart heavy. Come visit, come visit, she repeated, come out west. But I'll be back. I'm sure.

On some of her final days there, she skidded down the vine-tangled bank of Duck Hollow, wove through the brush, balanced stone by stone as far as she could out into the deep blue body. She crouched down, down, down until she was level with the surface, until the sweep of unknown turned to a thin, hard line. The young woman held a great sigh, in and out. There, in a morning blushed in spring and silent save for the wash of a shallow river, she found the weight of her goodbyes. And she found it was a weight she could pack back into the mountains herself.

Here's one last story the young woman tried in Pittsburgh—she was a fish out of water. But now that home holds her, she still has an appetite for food that makes her thirsty. The list on scraps of lined paper rests somewhere in boxes she's yet to unpack. Really, when it comes down to it, the young woman was a bird in a river. A true Yinzer, a friend there once told her, never settles for Heinz on their fries.

•

A friend at work tells the young woman of a small-engine plane that supposedly crashed and burst to shrapnel in the cliffs above Worden Lake in the Rattlesnake. On one hitch they pull out binoculars and sweep the rock face, sunlight blinking striations onto the slopes. Wouldn't that be something, they say, if there were scraps left to rust through winter. Back and forth they squint, and they wonder if the folklore had any merit—was it north or northwest of the lake? For all their scoping, it's the wrong angle to search. They come up empty.

There are plenty of tall tales. Sightings of the Flathead Lake monster, the lady in white of Chico Hot Springs, promises of gold shimmering up the next gulch. On their early-morning trek towards McLeod Peak, the young woman's boss tells her another story. Once that same packer hauled a full upright piano into a guard station in the Bob because the ranger's wife couldn't stand the silent summers without it. Or maybe she couldn't stand the ever-swishing river, grasshoppers chattering through dry bunchgrass, geese honking far too early in the autumn. Maybe, like her, this woman needed music almost as much as mountains, a key shift to make sense of her days.

The packer paced his corrals, the story goes, found his strongest mule, and fashioned up a pulley system to lower the piano onto her wide back. For the whole trip, the boss tells the young woman, the packer stopped every couple of miles and set up a high tripod that temporarily took the weigh off the mule. And the mule stood there, flicked long ears free of gnats, and took one enormous breath, in and out. Then the piano was lowered again, and they moved forward down the trail.

It's bright enough now that the young woman can catch the smirk on her boss's face. This is his last trek in Montana for some time; in a week he'll board a plane east, relocate to Maine with his family. As a parting gift he'll give the her a book coauthored by the famed packer of these stories, who, it turns out, isn't quite such an old-timer and lives in Missoula now, somewhere in the Rattlesnake Valley. She'll flip through the pages and read of diamond hitches and D-rings and manties, smile at black-and-white photographs of the packer hefting up perfectly balanced loads.

The young woman looks out at the open stands of ponderosa pine they pass, the gray cliff bands smoothed into this ancient glacial valley. She thinks of all the tales and knowledge her boss has accumulated through his work, sign and tool maintenance and shortcuts to barely touched basins. He was the one who taught her how to sharpen an ax, navigate off trail, know a place in all its idiosyncrasies. He had started to teach her different kinds of knots.

For a moment she shifts her perspective, taking on her boss's viewpoint of leaving. It rings with a flare of familiarity. And all at once, like a rush of downpour, she falls for the place all over again, misses it with a wild, profound ache, even though she'll be back next weekend, and the weekend after that.

She remembers when she did leave, for Pittsburgh and the times before. Attachments stretched thin like dry rubber bands, and her desperation each time she returned to find the grip slack. Somewhere in those months of overcast and languid rivers and forest canopies like branching lungs, those bands snapped. And maybe, she thinks—as great tamaracks heft above her, a handful of cold nights from easing into their golden suits—maybe it was best those links broke, if only because they were never sturdy in the first place.

The summer leans on, and when she returns from backcountry hitches, the young woman chops fresh herbs and slices potatoes in her kitchen, pulled every night to smudge dirt from their grainy skin. Outside the front windows Rattlesnake Creek hums through cottonwoods. Whitetail deer nudge into the neighbor's apple trees. There's word that great gray owls are nesting somewhere in the silver-tipped canopy.

There are tall tales just about anywhere the young woman goes. She'd like to believe them, but sometimes she focuses on the thing that sticks out and overlooks the balance that's already there. Putting trust in a string of words is like leading a string of mules upriver. Spook one and the whole line goes askew.

The young woman would like to believe there are secrets we only catch out of the corner of our eye. Mysteries swaddled in black water, narratives never cut into checkerboards. She doesn't know if the ketchup squeeze bottle was born in the Bob, something so emblematic in that messy wildness, a family saga altered by backcountry wit, as her boss's story goes. For the young woman, it was a connecting thread spanned between places she couldn't connect in herself. Maybe it's okay if that line has gone slack too.

But she'd like to believe the B-25 bomber did vanish. Not because the US Army had national security secrets onboard, not because it curled like a sleeping salamander in a gravel pit, but because the river swallowed the whole plane away piece by piece. She wants to believe that the Mon, for so long leaden with polluted metals, knew something of hunger, of reclamation.

Forget dirt-bound connections, purging downpours, a hankering for a food to replace a place. Take that list and pack it away, take a long cold swim. Maybe the young woman was meant to walk those years off-kilter. After all, the elk and owls and mules know it best, hairpin tracks and idiosyncratic skulls and long loops to end up right back where they started. There's no fault in overextension. That's how you fall for something. And the young woman learned this, just one thing—that's how you know what will then hold you.

PART II

POINT OF RETURN

7

Porcupine Ridge

Every time I drive past these meadows, my heart banks a little to the west, a left tilt as if aligning itself plumb. Pines the color of faded brick stand across the corridor of green where elk and moose forage. All around is old timberland, wiggling lines of firs sprouting from the clear-cut scars. Logging roads web the mountainsides into a maze, signage sparse, memory essential.

Once a homestead, the clear-cuts pardoned this old-growth ponderosa savanna. Trunks rise into pillars above flaxen bunchgrass, creeping Oregon grape, arrowleaf balsamroot, I imagine. The ecology is conjecture. I've never been down there, only turned my eyes through flashing alder as I pass. One of these days, I assure myself. It's on my list. Another wooded corner of the world to poke through, scratch my legs through snowberry, gulp the vanilla air. One of these days.

The Forest Service rig rattles on. I hang my arm out the window, return my eyes to the road. And miles to go, I think. And miles to go.

•

Monday evening, and the ER is quiet. I'm fine with that. I'd rather not be here, but for workers' compensation I have to go to a hospital before a regular doctor's office. I don't sit long in the waiting room, where it's just me and a woman in capri sweatpants crying on the phone.

"She's never been this sick," she says, wiping her nose. "I don't know what I'm doing wrong."

•

I carry the names in my mouth like warm stones. West Fork of Gold Creek. Bull Lake. Trail 333. Boulder Point. Five Lakes Basin. Trail 518. Fly Lake. Trail 504. Triangle Peak. Porcupine Ridge.

I close my eyes and see them. I open my eyes and see them, gleaming in the post-storm light. I open a map and trace them under my fingertips.

Where to next.

•

The nurse traces the swollen back of my ankle. "Do you remember a specific moment of injury?" he asks.

I could bore him with the specifics. A thousand feet climbing out of Boulder Lake, cutting out a seventeen-inch diameter rotten ponderosa across the trail with a crosscut saw. Then twenty-five hundred feet down Porcupine Ridge, sawing out another eighteen-inch fir. Thirteen miles that day, most with a sixty-five-pound pack. The last five miles felt like a stone had tucked itself against my heel.

I shake my head. "I couldn't say. It just got increasingly worse."

He nods and has me turn over onto my stomach so he can squeeze my calf. "You're all good there, at least," he says.

I think of the white strip of tendon that roots at the ankle and runs up my leg, like a limber trunk branching into sunset-red muscle.

•

The red-tailed hawk screams above the trail junction. She was screaming there a week ago, and the week before that. The word *scream* fits the sound, but I'm not sure the emotion holds. She could be singing.

"Sick of this trail yet?" I ask my crew member. She shrugs.

We hang a right onto Trail 518. I haven't been on this stretch in four years. Still I can count the dips in the trail, the shaded flat bench leading to our camp spot.

On the tread, moose tracks split through mud. Behind one, the faint print of a wolf. Dense claws spur into the dark loam.

I hover my fingertips over the print and ground them softly into the pads. The earth feels warm, but then again, all earth feels warm after a storm.

The air smells like rain and hunger.

•

In the curtained-off area next to mine, the baby has stopped crying. She's stopped throwing up, and her fever's come down, I hear the mother in capri sweatpants say, down from 103. Her voice still chokes.

"I don't know what's going on with my allergies," she says, and sniffs. "God, this never happens. I took allergy pills and everything."

Above my bed, painted fish twist against the wall. The mural stops at eye level, so that the beige paint job turns to sand. There are no windows in the ER unit. I've been outside for four days straight, where there are no windows because everything is a window. I feel like I'm underwater.

The mother flashes out of the room, dabbing her eyes. A man emerges from behind a curtain holding the baby. He has a buzzcut and tattooed arms and a beer gut. The baby lies across his stomach, left arm draping down his side. She's asleep, and the man watches her face.

He looks up at me with a broken grin. "Advantage of a belly," he says, swaying side to side under the fluorescent lights.

•

We take lunch on the steep ridge above Boulder Lake, where snowbanks slump in waves beneath whitebark pines. A cold wind spikes sunlight across the rocks, distinctly un-summer-like. Today is the first day of July. I slip numb hands into my down coat.

Gold Creek Basin. McLeod Peak. Across the Jocko, the Mission Range, shawled in snowfields. The Swan Range above the Clearwater River. One of those high peaks blinking white in the Scapegoat is Red Mountain, but I'm not sure which one. My maps don't go that far. Some day. It's on my list.

Below me is a sheer drop of five hundred feet. Subalpine fir and whitebark snags jut into the sharp brushes of wind, and from up here they look like long emerald feathers dipped into the earth. I shift my shoulders back into the cold stone, ignoring the jab of bedrock. When I nod off I dream of these same places.

•

Above me the vitals monitor asserts a high beep. I never got hooked up, and the screen shows a green thread sunk to the base, flatlining.

The little girl fidgets, scrunches her face.

"There, there, I know," the man says. "She's not even mine," he adds, looking at me past the curtain. "But damn. Today it sure feels like it."

•

Porcupine Ridge is the Great Divide of the Rattlesnake. Its northeast flank drops water into West Fork Gold Creek, to Gold Creek, to the Blackfoot River. In the southwest, Porcupine Creek draws it down Rattlesnake Creek to the Clark Fork River. The waters touch again in town, just downstream of the footbridge strung in globe lights that wink against gusts of Hellgate wind.

We march down the ridge, finally shedding our down jackets as the clouds skim south. I wander off trail to pee and follow the narrow tread of a game trail, or an old stock trail. I find a blaze in a tree, bark scraped to the soft, pitchy cambium. It could have been hatched from a single bit, or bruised from another tree toppling down beside it, or a bull elk rubbing his antlers during rut. I think about following the trail until it threads out, swallowed by huckleberry bushes, sunk into headwater springs that tip water one way or the other.

We still have seven miles to go until camp. I turn back down the game trail, away from another wooded corner of the world I've yet to touch.

•

The radiologist is lanky with kind eyes. When I sit up to follow him, he smiles and stops me. "You just lay back," he says, stomping the brakes on the bed's wheels.

I can walk fine. I walked fine four miles this morning, albeit in sandals because my sturdy Italian leather boots sent my whole lower leg throbbing. Still, the radiologist pushes me through the quiet ER. I fold my hands over my stomach, which curves hollow beneath my palms.

"Who'd you kick?" the man holding the baby asks me as I'm wheeled past.

"Just myself," I say.

•

The US Geological Survey map I carry on this hitch won't make it out again, soaked in drizzle one time too many. It's eighteen years old. The edges feather out, and its creased corners have yawned into star-shaped holes.

Just east of the wilderness boundary, there's a lake split in half by the map's edge, labeled Hidden Lake. One side is ringed in contour lines, splashed with the green wash of timber, and the other side lies blank. No texture or color save for the paper's stain, a blotch of soil that needled into the fibers and settled there like red algae in snow.

Where to next.

•

Outside of dentist's visits, this is my first x-ray. Childhood spared me broken limbs besides a cracked tailbone and, so far, so has this line of fieldwork. The radiologist drapes a heavy blanket across my lap and clicks a gridded light onto my ankle. He steps behind a small partition. Through the window I can see his face and the computer screen gathering images of my foot. White stones pressed with precision onto a bed of graphite. Ligaments like spiderwebs yoked to the tarsals.

I picture the pile of scat we passed the day before, from a coyote or small wolf, knotted with grainy hair. It was fresh enough that flies hummed away as I crouched down. Shards of bone poked through, gnawed keen and smooth.

After the long winter, maybe the canine was desperate. I can see him trotting across a moose calf that didn't make it through the snowpack, tearing into blizzard-tough hide to the ulnas and vertebrae still cold as ice.

Or, I remember, maybe it was a feast. Fatty marrow husked in ossein, lapped out with a hungry ruby tongue. The hidden places. This is where the good stuff sinks, dark and rich, down a long corridor of bone.

•

At the base of Porcupine Ridge, I throw my pack down in the shade of a ponderosa. The trail peters out into a rocky wash. Spotted knapweed grips between sprigs of yarrow and wild strawberry.

I pace the wash, back and forth, one heavy foot placed carefully in front of the other. My fingers lift the three-lobed strawberry leaves one by one by one. Eyes search for crimson-fruited stars hidden in green and stone.

I've scoped too many miles to count, too many places to name. The distances have worn me thin. This is all I want right now, a blink of blood-red, a sweetness drawn from the sun.

I find two berries. I hand the ripe one to my crew member. The other rests pale in my fingers, pricked with graphite-gray seeds, flesh rolling from white to blush like a sunset. In my mouth it's as tart as rain.

•

The radiologist figures my ankle looks fine. "I'll get those images to the doctor," he tells me, lifting the leaden cover from my lap. He unlocks the bed's brakes again and throws his weight into the frame. Back we go down the empty corridor, past whiteboard charts scribbled with names and areas of focus. *Debbie, pelvis. Allen, shoulder. Michael, thoracic.* The bed rumbles across polished linoleum, thunder hemming a valley.

We roll through a tight corner where one edge juts into the hallway. Even though I've never run a river, I'm reminded of shooting a raft past canyon walls. There's a hand's length of clearance on either side of the bed rails. The radiologist barely adjusts.

"You've really got that spot down," I say.

He laughs. "Eighteen years," he says, wheeling me back into the triage unit where the man and woman are packing up to take their baby home. "Eighteen years and that corner has never changed. I could do it with my eyes closed."

•

I count my corners, the sway between their margins. They are walls of granite and timber frayed in snow. They don't change much either, but still fires burn and limestone topples and trails sink beneath jackstraws of pine.

If I close my eyes, I can see them, curtained in mist, bronzed in sunset, coiled out across a tattered map and inked in names.

If I close my eyes, I miss the changing light. The fluorescent light. I miss these hidden places, the long corridors of beige, the baby asleep and cool and held by arms inked in names.

•

I haven't yet figured out the irony of this injury. Achilles' heel, a spot of weakness, of vulnerability. A swollen tendon, a jaw-gnawed bone, a tree skinned to cambium. A lake orphaned of its shoreline.

No long distances for one week, the doctor writes on my discharge forms.

I limp back outside into the evening light. To the north Porcupine Ridge hooks a final slab of sunset.

Someday I'll place the irony. One of these days. I've moments and miles to go.

8

Different Kinds of Solitude

Where Cinnamon Bear Creek stumbles into Rock Creek, things start to disappear.

The first is a ford—shallow and cobbled sweep of Rock Creek where it's only possible to wade across in late summer. There's a brush-knit path more akin to a game trail that skirts off from the road, and it slumps around ponderosas and ashy-leaved cottonwoods before opening to the bouldered shore of Rock Creek. An old wood sign nailed to a tree names the access point—*FORD*—with an arrow etched straight ahead.

Straight across the creek, though, there's no matching sign, no continuation of Trail 93 that weaves the ridgetop all the way to Cinnamon Bear Point. Just thicker dogwood and willow and pockets of humped grass where bears like to nap—the southern tip of the Welcome Creek Wilderness, which stretches just under thirty thousand acres north from this point in the shape of a ragged heart.

The ford across Rock Creek into the wilderness doesn't disappear entirely. There is a paired sign on the opposite bank, but it's nailed into a big old pine about a hundred yards upstream, like the whole Welcome Creek Wilderness slid south on a nonexistent fault line. Things in Welcome Creek don't disappear completely. They shift and hide and dart and slip into mats of stinging nettle and fireweed and currant brambles. Sometimes you have to walk right over them three times before they show up. Parts go missing, but the whole is always there.

Sometime in the tail end of the 1800s, white prospectors panning in the area pried a scuffed gold nugget from bedrock, and when they weighed it, the scale tipped 1.5 pounds. The record holds as one of the largest bodies of gold ever found in the state, and rumors took like cheatgrass. Ramshackle men came snooping up the sparkling waters of Welcome Creek, shoveled into ravine flanks to carve out foundations, felled lodgepole and ponderosa to notch into squat cabins. They collected flecks of gold and jealousy. There were scuffles, grudges, shoot-outs. The terrain, dry and steep like the hatch marks of an ax thrown into wood, won't let anyone stay long. Most of the rocks only sparkle with fool's gold and reek of stale gunpowder. Mining equipment rusted, cabins dipped swaybacked.

People still pan the notched creeks with names like Spartan, Ferret, Solomon, even though prospecting is prohibited under Forest regulations. They're searching for the missing pieces of that larger golden whole, a sign staggered across a border of water.

Welcome Creek, an old boss told me often, is a different kind of solitude.

•

Any northbound ravine spurring up from Welcome Creek's namesake stream is as good as any other. My coworker Melanie and I eye the gunmetal-gray tumble of talus above us, already sweating under the pale sky. There's no wind here in the gully bottom, though I know there will be up on the ridge where we're headed, the kind of directionless bluster that always leaves hair in your face. We eye some of the spurs of dusty soil beside the talus field, still opt for the shifting stones. With sections of the slope rearing close to forty-five degrees of exposure, an eight-pound block of lichen-edged bedrock feels like a safer bet than three inches of loose sandy soil where juniper bushes are barely hanging on.

We've been trying to get to the abandoned camp two thousand feet up this ridge for two years, a project booted down the program of work partly by an intern dropping out and bursitis in my heel, but mostly by the nature of the camp. In the office I share with Melanie, the trail crew, and sometimes the Forest's social outreach coordinator, it's scribbled on my seasonal to-do whiteboard under a different name—*fatality camp*. For that I was grateful for the tardy intern, the lump of swollen bursa at the base of my right leg. I kept making up projects to do instead.

In summer of 2014 a hunter was scoping out shelved ridges below a known saddle and came across a camp staked in the middle of nowhere. A dozen yards off any trail in Welcome Creek feels like the middle of nowhere, but this location was particularly far flung, two thousand vertical feet and miles from any water source, with no easy access by trail or even an easy ridge walk. The camp, the hunter noticed, was a strewn and shredded jumble of empty cans and gear. And then he saw other parts scattered around the camp.

Later that week the hunter returned to the crag-topped site with officers from the county sheriff's department, plus some medical and field evacuation personnel, to remove the body. It had been there for a couple of years, the county coroner decided, and there wasn't much to go off. No ID or personal items, just a menagerie of hunting and camping gear, a wind-shredded single-person tent.

The crew that packed out the deceased individual left what wasn't evidence, which ended up being most of the abandoned camp. Whatever remained went back to the responsibility of the Missoula Ranger District, a project bumped from one summer to the next, until Melanie and I managed to get to it on our third try. Or, at least, we've so far made it four hundred vertical feet closer than the past two attempts.

Reaching the tops of the jostling talus fields doesn't make the slope any less abrupt. I opt for a furrow in the terrain, almost a cut bank, that spills into a scree field, and pull myself up by loops of ponderosa roots somehow holding out on this arid aspect. There are spindly grasses latched into the thin topsoil too, and clumps of them tip downward in dusty tumbles under my feet.

The wind starts to drift between the hatched drainage. Below me Welcome Creek and its scarf of dogwood and willow and stinging nettle drops out of claustrophobic immediacy. Upstream the creek bed makes halting turns to the north, jostled behind cliffs the color of dried pitch. I suck in a breath and exhale; Melanie pauses on the other side of the talus field, catching hers. Above us the ridge looks like it tops to sky in a few hundred feet, but we both know that's not the case. It's one of those slopes too steep for line of sight, a shove of dry mountain that decided it wanted little to do with the curvature of the earth.

•

The first time I stepped into Welcome Creek was the same summer the hunter stumbled across the fatality camp. By the end of the day, a sixteen-mile haul to pack out a purposefully abandoned hunting camp, I had second-degree blisters ringing both ankles. My coworker at the time managed to break a toe.

Two summers later, my first as lead ranger, my crew and I were driving to the wilderness from its northwest side when our truck got a flat. We pulled apart the cab looking for a lug wrench that wasn't there. I got a hold of the trail crew lead on the satellite phone, who got a hold of a coworker who usually staffed the front desk, who drove two hours through the maze of clear-cut logging roads towards Welcome Mountain only to get a flat about a mile from where we were stranded.

Welcome Creek likes to keep things, or else people like to stash things and then forget about them. Rusted bars from mining equipment jut from the ground like ribcages. Bear hunters dig pits for their skinning knives and water jugs and canvas tents, and then don't come back. Turn a corner on the trail and a cabin slumps into the needle-soft earth, time suspended alongside kettles and ladles and washpans above the low doorframe. All these scattered pieces of stories that don't sit right. I tell myself I don't much believe in ghosts, but there's unfinished energy cleft in the gullies here, land too steep for sunrise or sunset. The sky just pales, and darkens, and speckles as cold air rushes over sunbaked stones.

•

Melanie and I make it to a bench on the ridge crest where dry fists of creeping Oregon grape crunch under our boots. The slope softens enough for the grass to spread from bunched wads to pockets of meadow, and I wonder if there's an unmapped spring nearby. We chug water and I check the GPS—not even halfway up.

The view from here has started widening to something of a panorama, steep hillsides on the other side of Welcome Creek glinting with snags that burned in 2007. It's hard to tell, but the whole wilderness burned that year, mountainsides left scabby with mismatched hotspots. The fire wormed into the bases of the trees and then moved on, so that over a decade later they're still toppling during wind storms, or else waiting for the drop of a chickadee to snap and slide like a bobsled two hundred yards through crashing scree.

Here there are hardy ponderosa pines that barely show any fire scars, and they add vanilla and butterscotch to the breeze cooling our backs. Melanie points out pellets of elk scat on the ground. Where the summer-yellow grass is thickest, I can catch the faintest scent of the herd's musk, notice the gentle impressions their bodies left in the leaves.

•

I had one good hitch in Welcome Creek, three days camped at Carron Cabin about five miles up the main drainage. Sawing lodgepole with the crosscut still felt more like sawing hardwood, but there weren't any notable injuries, lost tools, trails disappearing into a wall of self-pruning firs. A dry lightning storm rolled through on the last night, bouncing cracks of thunder down the canyon. I lay awake in my sleeping bag and counted the seconds between flashes of light and ground-rooted booms, none less than five seconds. The air, dry and electric, took on the smell of gunpowder.

My crew and I came out of that hitch on June 12th, 2016. The flatbed I'd been assigned that season, a Chevy crew cab manual rife with mechanical problems, bumped down the washboards of Rock Creek Road, and when we hit I-90 west back towards Missoula, the dust slunk into the rearview mirror. A broad plane of sky stretched overhead, skimmed by harmless clouds.

I was driving back from the office when I turned my phone on and saw my mom's text. Idling at North Reserve and Mullan Road, named for and following the historic tracks of the first wagon route built by white settlers between Fort Benton and Walla Walla, authorized in 1853 as an arm of military expansion to continue displacing the Yakima and other tribes, I read that the United States had just witnessed its worst mass shooting in modern history. The same time lightning seamed the sky over Welcome Creek, a rattle of gunfire echoed, disjointed, across swamp and longleaf pine forest and prairie and plateau and mountaintop.

I stared through the intersection at an American flag at the Conoco shrugging in the wind. To this day I couldn't tell you whether or not it was already at half-staff.

•

A group of Vikings, the story goes, took off from Norway and stumbled across then-unnamed Iceland. Looking over the coastal hillsides dabbed in soft moss, they fretted that their rivals would stake a claim on the puffin-guarded land as well. So they sent word back of the bleak beach where they'd landed, Iceland, and of another landscape farther to the northwest that sparkled green across the northern ocean. Maybe, they thought, their rivals would skim past their secret discovery for a place as enticing as one called Greenland.

The story isn't quite true. Someone from Norway did crash into the coarse sand of Iceland's shoreline during the 9th century, but the weather was characteristically bad and when the wind-sharp squalls did clear, half the horizon stretched into domes of glacial ice. The next person to investigate was a Swede, whose vessel slipped between icebergs bobbing in the surf. Iceland was never named to hide anything, never took a title as a trickster.

Greenland is different. Moving on from Iceland, Norwegians then came across another mass of land they decided to claim, despite the fact that Inuit civilization had been around far longer than their boom and bust empires. Hoping to encourage more settlers, they changed Kalaallit Nunaat to Greenland, a name whittled to subterfuge.

I worked four years on the Missoula Ranger District, patrolling its two wilderness areas—the Rattlesnake and Welcome Creek. Experience has put them in the camp of the Iceland/Greenland naming myth, one named to deter from a hidden grandeur, the other to draw people into something deemed to have little worth. The Rattlesnake doesn't have any rattlers, just glossy alpine lakes and long valleys soothed by glaciers and broad sunsets pricked by swallows over the mist-smudged water. Welcome Creek has no lakes. Its greenery stings and tears clothes, snatches pencils and plastic wedges from pockets. It's a place, I've found, steeped in flat tires and pinched crosscut saws, radio and satellite phone signals bouncing feebly over the Sapphire Divide. A place of misguided luck, as if a pound and a half of solid gold was all the mountains wanted to offer, and from there all the good luck ran dry.

The catch, though, is that neither Iceland or Greenland or the Rattlesnake or Welcome Creek are boxed into black or white. The

Rattlesnake wore down my knees and flared that bursitis; Greenland had been perfectly habitable for thousands of years without a name that tricked people into thinking they could grow tomatoes north of the Arctic Circle.

I don't know why Welcome Creek is called Welcome Creek. Or more specifically, I'm never sure who the welcome is for. On its southeast border, there's a simple name tacked into a cottonwood on Rock Creek's east side—*FORD*, and it's both a lie and a promise once you reach the other side.

•

I check the GPS again. We've climbed two thousand feet of elevation in three-quarters of a mile. There's a definite ridge crest up ahead, a blocky outline of a bluff between slats of pines, no trickery of perspective this time. The trepidation kicks in. I don't like forgotten things. I don't like stumbling into a story doused in violence. I don't like thinking about the last pair of hands to put up the threadbare tent, click sections of metal into two arcing poles.

In another three hundred feet, we reach the bluff, and Welcome Creek jumps into view again below us, a staggered curve of green against unforgiving stone. The wind tries to take my hat, and Melanie dabs on more sunscreen. The faintest tread of a trail meanders uphill, parallel to the crest, impossible to tell between a game trail or human-stamped path. Melanie shrugs, and we follow it upslope, winding around limestone boulders and wind-warped ponderosas. I glance at the GPS, digital compass pegged to the camp's location—two hundred feet away.

We both agree we thought it would be easy enough to find. And we both forgot we were in Welcome Creek, where nothing is transparent or forthcoming, even a camp on a ridge that's barely wide or flat enough to pitch a tent on. Where the GPS says I'm standing right on top of the coordinates, I'm balanced on a rocky overhang, the mountain pitching downslope at an angle that twists my stomach. Melanie and I pace back and forth on the hump of ridge for twenty minutes. Maybe, I wonder, the abandoned camp took care of itself.

And then Melanie finds it, right there in plain sight, popping into view like huckleberries when you finally notice them. There are shredded bits of clothes and shattered glass pockmarking the ground, a drape of rope drifting from a tree branch. A hunting knife, handsaw, lighter, more clothes, one leather glove. A slumped tent so sun-bleached it's barely any color at all. Wrapped around a rough trunk, a sleeping bag, ripped and gutted and limp.

"Who would come all the way up here?" Melanie asks. She's usually the one to jump right into a job, no hesitation, but for a moment we both stand there, staring. "Why?"

There's only the faintest ghost of an old despair here. I don't feel like I'm violating anyone's secrets anymore; that energy sloughed away with the wind a long time ago. There are only things, disjointed, unravelling back into the earth. I put on my work gloves and start taking apart what's left of the single-person tent.

•

Early in the morning of June 12th, 2016, a young man walked into the Pulse Nightclub in Orlando, Florida, and opened fire on the crowd of over three hundred people with a semiautomatic rifle and a semiautomatic pistol. It was Latinx night at the queer club, not long after the bartenders had announced last call. Fifty-one people, including the shooter, were killed, making it the deadliest episode of violence against the LGBTQ community in US history.

These were the stories that stuck with me, those numb days after I got back from Welcome Creek—the cell phones of those shot ringing and ringing and ringing on the blood-smeared dance floor. Strewn shoes and shattered margarita glasses and limp coats and chairs belly-up. First responders walking through the bullet-torn space to a desperate, glaring silence; what would they say if they picked up a phone and answered? People went into that club and shed their facades with the bouncer, and then they were outed by their own deaths.

I couldn't stop thinking about the outings. I couldn't stop thinking about the pieces we carry around inside of us, shame that doesn't need to be shame, staggered stories that change depending on which shore you're standing. I couldn't stop thinking about all the shame I'd stuffed like a down sleeping bag into my chest, or how my impulse to keep others away from those scars put me in these places of exposure and heat stroke and grizzlies and armed men and hypothermia and terrain that shrugs off the earth's dome. I couldn't stop thinking about those phone calls.

As candles and letters and bundles of flowers gathered against the sidewalks in Orlando, I drove home, back east on I-90 past the Rock Creek exit to flash beside the Clark Fork, then the Little Blackfoot, then over MacDonald Pass where the snowfields still gleamed like glaciers. I sat my parents down on the back porch of the house my brother and I grew up in, and in the backyard the row of Russian olives were just blooming, flushing the air with the smell of sweet oranges.

I remembered the unanswered cell phones on the club floor. Anything could happen. I remembered the forms I filled every year working for the Forest Service, the blank boxes for how to reach my next of kin. I remembered coming out to my best friend earlier that spring, how later we went dancing in a club that was a family Mexican restaurant by day. Anything, no matter the place, but especially in this place, could happen.

•

A road engineer from the Lolo National Forest office happened to be out scoping the same road that had pierced not one, but two all-terrain tires on the scribbled northwest border of Welcome Creek below Welcome Mountain. She was checking out a spot not half a mile from our slumped rig where the roadbed itself was slumping downslope, and eased her two-person truck to a stop in front of us.

Our coworker from the front desk came walking up the road not long after, bemused at the whole situation, packing a lug wrench and extra jack. The nuts on the flatbed's tires, it turned out, were wound so tight that not even the weight of a full-grown man jumping on the wrench could budge them. We unloaded our gear, defeated, and stuffed packs and tools and ourselves into the covered bed of the tiny pickup, crept back down the road as if there were shards of glass glinting among the dust.

We were lucky. We got the other truck's flat changed and made it back only slightly before dark. The next day I went back up the labyrinth of logging roads with a guy from the trail crew blessed with a knowledge of machinery I couldn't pretend to understand. We stopped at O'Reilly Auto Parts on our way out of town and used the agency credit card to buy a cross wrench and a can of rust-stripping chemicals.

Back at the abandoned flatbed, we blasted the lug nuts in an aerosol that smelled like fermented oranges. The pieces of metal loosened, released, spun into my palms, viscous and warm.

•

That first trip into Welcome Creek, I wore the wrong kind of socks, a mesh hiking pair that only stretched up to my ankles. The exposure, coupled with sodden boots from a rain-drenched underbrush, polished sticky-damp fabric across skin just as damp. I ignored the building pain until, fourteen miles later, I remembered I had a pair of dry, calf-high socks stashed in my pack. By then, it was too late. The fabric of my boot cuffs had chaffed through epidermis to the tender dermis layer of my skin, a ring of raw wounds around each ankle.

Back in town I wouldn't let anyone within a couple feet of me. It was instinctual, animal, a relentless drive to shield the blood-dappled blisters. At night I slept with my calves propped on rolled-up towels so that my ankles hung free without any points of contact. I got unnerved at how quickly I flinched away from people, how the cuffed scars lingered for years.

Maybe it was the distance from people and objects, or maybe just luck, but I managed to avoid an infection. The wounds flushed ruddy, then drained something that wasn't blood. It was the color, almost, of gold.

•

We fit all the abandoned belongings into a handful of fifty-gallon black plastic bags. Rusted carabiners, scraps of sleeping pad, frayed blue tarp, broken tent poles tugged from the earth like arrows. Everything gets wrapped up and cinched against our own packs, swinging side to side regardless. We stop at the bluff again to take a late lunch, peer down at Trail 225 meandering northwest a vertical mile below.

"How do you think they got up here?" Melanie asks. "I can't imagine lugging all of this up from down there."

"Maybe from the west, then," I offer, picturing the flat ridge climbing northeast towards the center of the wilderness's heart. "They could have driven all the way up from Swartz Creek. But then that's miles and miles off trail with no sure water source."

"Wouldn't someone have noticed the vehicle?" Melanie says. "Even if they'd parked in a hidden pullout? There are firewood cutters, hunters, road engineer crews up there all the time."

"It's hard to believe no one came to look for them after they disappeared," I say. The wind snatches at my hat again. "Wouldn't someone have noticed they were gone?" I think of how things slip out of sight in Welcome Creek, of the hairpin road that zigzags to the base of Welcome Mountain, the same road that punctured the flatbed's tires. Someone found us that day.

The county's investigation into the camp, as far as I knew, never lead to any answers. Melanie and I sit on the outcrop puzzling through place names, hung up on the logistics of *how*. We pace around the *why*, the isolation and a death no one seemed to notice. Those pieces are too tender to touch.

I wish I could leave something at the camp, a scratch of limestone on slate, a single glove tangled in beargrass. It's not so much guilt as a fear of complete erasure, like we've bundled the last of this stranger's secrets in plastic bags without knowing how they wanted them to be found out.

Still, there are paintbrushes in bloom. White-tipped heads of elk sedge, heart-leafed arnicas glowing like sunrise. Bundles of creeping Oregon grape whose waxy leaves will stay green all winter, only flushing crimson when the snow starts to melt away.

•

I once spent ten days in Iceland on a grad school field seminar, and we landed into a steel-gray landscape and skyline torn by wind. On the runway at Keflavík, I watched gray rain splatter into a mist on the tarmac, then realized it wasn't raining at all, just the wind shooting slabs of puddled water across the ground.

After that first day, though, the overcast slunk away and we woke to a still, cirrus-brushed sky. Boats wrangled tight into the harbor at Akranes wore sharp reflections in the water. The trend continued for the next week, blue-marble skies and no whisper of rain or ice-nipped storms. The locals shook their heads and pointed out, regularly, how lucky we were.

Iceland, true to its name, is pockmarked in glaciers. The tour bus lugged us past too many to count, and one blue-stamped day our group hiked to the retreating bulk of Sólheimajökull. I numbed my fingertips in its meltwater, sifted through the gritty slush of its calving flanks. One friend cupped her palms and brought the needle-cold water to her mouth.

Threading back down the trail among other tour groups, I remember our guide lifting her arm to a bare rock basin below the path. "This used to be the glacier," she said. "Ten years ago, it was right there." She pointed to a lone string of flags stretched across the middle of the flat scrape of earth, half a mile away from the melting gleam of Sólheimajökull.

This was the image that stuck with me—not so much the calving, slumping, dripping, puddling, grit-streaked heft of the glacial tongue, but the fluttering line of plastic flags staked too far away, much too far away, the empty valley where the glacier had disappeared, the grief of distance between them.

•

Melanie and I do a season's worth of damage to our knees on the way back down the ridge, but otherwise return to the trailhead in one piece. We took separate rigs to get here; I have another trail to patrol in the area tomorrow, and Melanie needs to be back in town. The black plastic bags go into the bed of her pickup, bound back to civilization.

As Melanie churns up dust north towards I-90, I head the other way, south on Rock Creek Road until I reach Dalles Campground. I unload my own gear—a fraying tarp, sleeping bag and pad, two-person tent with brand new tent poles after the previous pair cracked and split. I take off my uniform, shrug on a down coat and knit hat, fire up my camp stove and set aside some rice noodles to soak. Sunlight lifts off the craggy opposite bank of Rock Creek until it's only a brush of amber in the treetops.

I stir seasoning into the pot of noodles and prop open *Giovanni's Room*, James Baldwin's classic of queer literature. It's a compelling read, heavy with guilt and secrecy and shame; I dog-ear and underline the familiar echoes. The sky pales from its sun-struck blue to the color of goose down, then pricks with the evening's first stars. I turn the book's final pages in the waning light—the protagonist learns of his lover's death by firing squad, holds in his hands a blue envelope that names the date of execution. He tears the paper into pieces and watches the scraps loop away with the wind. The air shifts, bends the scraps back against him.

I click on my headlamp and crawl into my tent. Rock Creek hushes through dusk across the campground, and across the water the Welcome Creek Wilderness lifts into nightfall. Tomorrow I'll pack up all my things, drive down the washboarded road to a narrow pullout where a hint of a trail weaves into the underbrush. I'll roll up my pants and wade across the creek, then spend two hours searching for the trail that climbs to Cinnamon Bear Point, searching for the missing side of the ford.

Sometimes I can still make out the glossed scars around my ankles from the first time I stepped out of Welcome Creek. Whenever I share this anecdote, I tell the story as if it was the wilderness that scoured those wounds, not the other way around. I tell it as if I wasn't hurting the whole time, all sixteen miles, as if it were toughness that kept me going. I don't talk about the twisting, watered gaps of shame, how familiar all these scraps feel, how the air between them is both a balm and a buffer, a lie and a promise, a loss that stumbles into the golden whole.

I turn off the light. Starlight scuffs the dome of my tent, drawing its seams dark and crisp as stitches.

Postscript: This essay takes place in the summer of 2018 and was written in the spring and summer of 2020. The individual found at the camp has since been identified, but I have not included any further details out of respect for them and their family.

In 2020 the Cinnabar Fire burned much of the west-central area of Welcome Creek Wilderness, including much of the area described in this essay.

9

What Stones Hold

Only days later I'll remember the dull shift of rocks above Rattlesnake Creek where the roadbed cuts across steep talus. Sweat-slick palms on the steering wheel and gearstick, flush of electric adrenaline. Basalt or granite or limestone, the jostle of loose stones under any set of tires feels just about the same.

This isn't the first river channel we've forded today. The Markafljót River of southwest Iceland frays into spillways that tumble over black volcanic rock, around tussocks of golden grass and windblown brush. Meltwater rolls gravity-bound from marbled glaciers to the south and east—Eyjafjallajökull and Myrdalsjökull—and the old Scania tour bus plows and dips into the runoff. Its engine and three pairs of tires growl us back onto dry road of hard-packed basalt.

Except this time. The volcanic stones lie with their darkness, promise a shallow ford in the river channel only to reveal a deeper hollow, and the left front tire of the bus plunges in.

The bus, full of twenty graduate students and two professors on a ten-day field seminar, tips and leans heavily upstream, inching its way towards a forty-five degree angle. I yank my earbuds out and brace against the seat in front of me. Seated on the bus's right side near the front, I can hear our guide Vigga and driver Omar shooting rapid Icelandic back and forth. I don't speak more than two words of the language, but I understand the gist.

The thing is, we're not going to die. The channel lapping closer to the tour bus's windows isn't any deeper than five feet; we're not going to sink into some black depths or flip downstream in throws of whitewater. At worst, gravity will pull the bus onto its side in a heaving splash, and twenty-two Americans and two Icelanders will topple against seat belts, windowpanes, each other. We'll get scratched and bruised and maybe a little wet, and climb out the door which is now a ceiling. We're all writers, and it's certainly something good to write about.

Rattled out of a horizontal mindset, some of my classmates behind me start to laugh, already snapping photos to document the event before it even resolves. I don't. I turn back to the front of the bus, eyes latched to Omar. His palms grip the steering wheel and gearstick as the bus shifts deeper into the river. I can hear the engine heaving below us, but Omar's face doesn't show much ease or worry. He simply operates one second to the next. I can feel the stones beneath us clunk and settle deeper against each other. The tires spin as if in slow-motion, still finding nothing to hold onto.

Our guide Vigga sends everyone to the right side of the bus. We buckle in, and I brace my legs, grip the seat in front. My teeth grind against each other, an echo of the tight clicks in the rocks below. The bus inches forward and rolls back, inches forward and holds. Omar jams the stick into reverse, catching momentum to run forward again. In this moment of lurching and leaning, I can't imagine the delicacy of his feet dancing between clutch and gas pedal and brake pedal—left foot lifts from the clutch, right foot snaps from brake and catches the roar of engine before it chokes out. That's the echo I won't place until later down the rough-stone road.

The rear end of the bus pivots deeper into the meltwater, then flounders against stones that suddenly hold. And just like that, we heave out of the water. Omar relaxes back into his seat, my classmates cheer and clap, and at the same moment that the front tire touches ground again and that relief drops through the bus, the whole two-minute experience seizes up inside me and breaks, a meltwater of adrenaline. The cartilage in my breastbone feels like it's hardened to bone. I hunch against the windowpane, struggling to breathe. I feel like breaking through the window, stumbling into the broad glacier valley to drench myself in the shallow black river.

When the volcano Eyjafjallajökull erupted in 2010, magma boiled down its white flanks and gouged new rifts into the landscape. Iceland lived up to its name as the land of fire and ice as the earth's hot core poured out against ancient glaciers, which sent floodwaters racing to the valley floors. "I barely recognize this place now," Vigga had told us at an earlier stop, arm stretched out over Gígjökull, one of Eyjafjallajökull's main tongues. Scuffs of volcanic grit covered the glacier, and as far as I could see there wasn't any moraine field below, just a wide basin of rough ebony sediment and iced runoff. All the sharp stones the glacier had pushed into its characteristic lip were torn away in the aftermath of the eruption. They rattled north, a roar of water and bits of earth, some as small as grains of ash, others the size of a tour bus.

The adrenaline, something like magma, carves its way out of my bloodstream. It builds behind basalt dams and foams ahead again in waves—complete stillness, rattling breaths. Like the floods of Eyjafjallajökull, I figure I just have to wait it out. The flow pours back into old channels of anxiety and dry riverbanks I decidedly forgot. I can't trace anything upstream today, but I have a sense of where they lead.

•

For a good chunk of my childhood, the only family car was a manual 1995 Jeep. It was forest green and demanded a new clutch every two or three years, and rather than pour another couple hundred dollars into it at the shop, my parents put up with the bad clutch as long as possible, which usually involved shifting straight from first gear to third. I've always been easily prone to motion sickness, and riding in the backseat, the lurch from straining engine to low acceleration spun my inner ear into that woozy, migraine type of nausea. As much as possible, including in winter, I rode with the window cranked down.

I started driver's ed classes the summer after I turned fourteen. The school district had decided teaching kids to drive manual proved too stressful and time intensive, and half the class already spent summers driving old flatbeds and tractors down rural backroads. My dad used to let my brother and me work the clutch when he drove, his feet stepping between pedals, telling us exactly when to punch into a higher gear.

My driver's ed instructor had also been my fourth- and fifth-grade teacher. His wardrobe of almost exclusively Hawaiian shirts matched his cool demeanor, and he regularly brought a newspaper on practice drives and asked us to stop at gas stations so he could pop inside and buy a to-go cup of black coffee. In the training car, a forgettable pale gold Buick or Saturn, we meandered figure eights through the school parking lot and took to quiet neighborhoods. Gradually the routes included busier streets, intersections with stoplights, the one on-ramp onto I-15 that had two merging lanes, maybe the only one in the state at that time. A safety break, more akin to a tractor pedal, jutted out beside the car's glove compartment.

For a learner's permit I needed to cobble together practice hours outside of class, a requirement that got a lot harder when my practice vehicle was more akin to a tractor. My parents alternated taking me down to the county fairgrounds, where I staggered from stop to first gear to second in the sunbaked gravel lots. I spluttered the engine out, ground the gears again and again. My parents tried their best not to flinch.

Whatever progress I made with the Jeep existed in a controlled environment—flat, open, vacant of other vehicles. In the real world there were other vehicles, and they moved. There were four-way stops and left-hand turns and hills, so many hills. I brushed off these challenges in an automatic, and I did get the hang of shifting, though still with consistent lurching, from a stop all the way to fourth gear on the Jeep. The only hitch was combining these environments, and there I was barely functional.

One afternoon my mom and I were returning from a practice drive in the empty parking lot of my high school. The only observers had been seagulls and the cross-country team flowing past, so my confidence had tipped onto the positive side. I coaxed the Jeep up residential blocks blissfully absent of stop signs, and then the stoplight on Prospect Avenue blinked to yellow, to red.

The general layout of my hometown of Helena is a decline towards the Missouri River ruffled by gulches with gold rush-era names like Last Chance and Grizzly—in short, short steep hills on top of a larger downhill plane. My family lived in the South Hills, on the high side of the valley, so anywhere we went—school, friends' houses, downtown—was always lower in elevation. This meant biking to school was quick and cold in the mornings, protracted and hot in the afternoons, and it meant that the hardest parts of practice drives was coming home.

Prospect Avenue, also named in the thick of that Manifest Destiny, runs east to west, so that any streets meeting it perpendicularly do so steeply. And that afternoon, both my legs punched into the clutch and brake pedal at the intersection of Roberts and Prospect, I felt blood empty from my head and hands, pooling into nausea somewhere in my gut. Another car rolled up behind me, much too close.

Going from a stop forward on an incline in any vehicle involves a bit of a lag, a moment where the weight of the vehicle overrides the strength of its engine. In an automatic, it's a small and simple moment, right foot switching from brake pedal to a little more on the gas, and then you're in the clear. With a manual, especially a 1995 Jeep with a questionable clutch to begin with, that override of gravity is less of a lag and more of a free fall.

The light over Prospect Avenue turned green. I eased my foot off the clutch, felt the Jeep begin to roll backwards with that sickening lurch. Adrenaline flushed my face and fingertips, hot and sharp. My right foot snapped from the brake pedal to the gas, a transition that ignored all the instruction of finesse my parents had taught me. I wanted off the road. I wanted out of this moment, cars honking behind me, lip of the flat avenue tauntingly close, my mom urging me from the passenger seat, where there was no safety brake.

So I didn't coordinate a smooth sweep between my feet like I'd been practicing for weeks on level gravel lots. I floored it, and we gunned through the intersection like a Harley. This time my mom did flinch.

I've heard that the draw to driving manuals is the control. People get hooked to the feel of guiding the vehicle through gears with their own hands and feet, with the low purr of fourth and fifth on the highway. I get that, sure. But I could never get my body to mirror that transition. I grew up riding bikes, horses, running the curves of those west-central Montana gulches—the complexity of gears behind a tangle of machinery was just too much. It was a different language I could never quite got a hold of.

I don't know if that painful, full-throttle lurch contributed at all to my parents' decision to buy a Subaru, an automatic, that next winter. My brother was only a year behind me in school, and I don't blame them for not wanting to go through the stress and tearful moments at intersections and damage to an already poorly functioning clutch all over again. I somehow scraped by with enough practice hours in the Jeep to get my learner's permit, and then I never got back into that driver's seat.

Driving the Subaru was a different language, and this time I got it. Dark rivers rippled beside roadways that curved with their flow. I felt the rise and fall of mountain passes, let myself skid through fresh snow on empty streets. My left foot simply rested, unused and content, and I learned to get lost in that movement.

•

The morning before we crawl up the Markarfljót River Valley, I wake up early, a quarter to five. Iceland squats just below the Arctic Circle, and at the start of May days stretch to fifteen hours of natural light, night a long twilight in between. I've been consistently exhausted the whole trip and know I should be sleeping more, but I also know that steep mountains rise above the town Laugarvatn, where we're staying, and that trails wind through birchwood just across the main road from the hostel. Hiking paths and forest have always been hard for me to turn down.

On the trip so far, I've only run roadways or boggy sheep trails, and there's little to call woodland in Iceland. When Norwegian settlers first came here in the ninth century, they built turf houses and burned cord after cord of birchwood to make it through the oppressively dark winters. Over time the forest cover of Iceland dwindled, leaving the island stark like a sheered sheep. *If you ever get lost in the woods in Iceland*, a saying goes, *just stand up*.

Against the lengthening days, spring is still a murmur from the south. I've seen the occasional green-thumbed bush or daffodil sprouts behind the windbreak of a stone wall, but this southeast corner of Iceland remains overwhelmingly held in the sepia in-between of winter and spring. Grass and moss carpeting the forest ebbs a faint green against umber birchwood not yet budded. A cool fog has swept up from the lake into the steep hills, and any color in the landscape is dabbed white.

I find the hiking path and take a slow jog into the mist. The truth is that even without access to soft-earthed trails, I would still get up at quarter to five and sprint circles around Laugarvatn if I had to. I've been running on a near daily basis for seven years now, and I've got something of a dependence on these morning shots of endorphins. Not to mention that here in Iceland, packed from place to place along with my twenty classmates, this quiet hour of only my breaths and heartbeat and quick feet keeps me sane, a reset of the days spent shuffling in and out of the Scania tour bus on a predetermined schedule.

Traveling in groups, at least to me, means giving up its main draw—the control of getting from one place to another on your own—which is equally its main stressor—the responsibility of getting from one place to another on your own. The fall after I graduated college, I took a three-month solo backpacking trip to Europe, which brought a lot of personal growth in hindsight and a whole lot of anxiety in the present moment. I got off trains at the wrong station, missed bus stops, found myself stranded at a gas station in the suburbs of Oslo with only Swedish krona in my pocket. Somehow I always slipped through, and whether it was luck or a budding intuition, that's what got me hooked.

This field seminar in Iceland promises the opposite. Days planned out, spontaneity as distant as full-fledged summer. Bags loaded into the bus by nine each morning, forty minutes to snap photos at a waterfall and try and place an impression of the landscape. I get there's just too much to tour in a country so scenic every view belongs on a postcard, vista stops hurried so we can see a diverse slice of Iceland, coast to farmland to snow-curtained passes. That what's proved to be the source of my underlying unease. For everything I see, there's not much I actually feel.

The trail climbs gradually through buff-colored forest, cutting through copses of pine and spruce. Laugarvatn fades into the fog below. I'm feeling lethargic, unhurried, content with an easy three-mile loop back to the main road. My stomach echoes empty, and I think about the Icelandic breakfast spread out in the hostel below—crisp *hrökkbrauð*, slices of cheese and tomato, carrot-orange and crowberry marmalades, muesli and skyr.

Just before the path I'm on curves downhill, the forest opens to a brushy ravine and stream trickling down its middle. I pause, glance up the slope. Another single track branches off the main trail beside the ravine, strung between posts of fluorescent squares. I consider the limitless cups of tea at the hostel's breakfast spread. Upslope the fog deepens. Even if I could see the rising mountain, I have no idea where the trail leads.

In the end, that's what tugs me uphill. I step off the moss-soft path onto the rocky trail, adjusting my pace to a power walk against the sharp slope. The track twists around stones burrowed into the ravine's floor before rising to sway parallel to its cutbanks. I keep climbing post to post. White fog muffles claps of closing doors and car engines down in Laugarvatn. The birch forest retreats into the smudged clouds.

I higher I push on, bushes and tussocks of grass disappear until it's only an occasional low shrub among rusty-black crumble of volcanic rock. It feels like a postcard scene that should snap into sharp contrasts—dark and edged terrain against the thick of clouds—but the fog sweeps a soft umber filter across the landscape so that there aren't any hard edges.

I stop at an outcrop overlooking the ravine. The slope rolls into a pointed cliff above like a wave breaking into fog. Movement catches my eye, a crisp white flash against the black ground, and a ptarmigan shuffles across the rocks in front of me. Still dressed in winter plumage, the bird stands out even against the pale backdrop of spilled overcast. Her tail ends in a black tip, small gray head pivoted in my direction. She picks her tufted feat across the ebony slabs and out of sight.

I keep climbing. I figure there's got to be a break in the clouds, some soft inversion pressing the moisture into the valley bottom while blue sky hangs above. Sometimes I think I see it, too, a daub the color of river ice, but it could just as well be a trick of vision. In the pale stillness of the morning, I can get a sense of exposure even without any views to bolster it. Later I'll look up the spread of landscape—Laugarvatn's huddle of buildings along the shore of its namesake lake, larger lake Apavatn to the southeast, quilted collection of farms and pastures eventually draining to the Hvítá River. In this drawn-out dawn, though, I don't see any of that. I don't see the postcard views or dots of Icelandic horses grazing against the wind or lava fields or valleys plowed flat by glaciers that sparkle on the horizon. I don't see all the terrain I'll never reach, no matter how early I pull myself out of bed or how far I run. I just have the spill and slide of pebbles beneath my feet, the rough catch of basalt bedrock.

Somehow the surrounding whiteness deepens. I realize that I might lose the reflective trail markers in the fog, that blue sky isn't just beyond the next post. I'm not too worried about getting lost, though descending off trail would prove to be a cumbersome ordeal, not to mention I'd probably miss breakfast. Time has worked its way back into my mindset. I let out a breath and stop, turn to take in the view that's no view at all, just a blank stretch of all things outside of my perspective. I squat down and cup the gritty soil in my palms, bring it to my face, and inhale the sharp mineral damp of the earth.

And then I pick my way back down the mountain.

•

A year before the Iceland trip, before I drove halfway across the country for grad school, I worked a season as the lead wilderness ranger based out of Missoula. I'd interned in the position two years prior, then did another internship in the Absaroka-Beartooth Wilderness, then spent the better part of half a year living out of a sixty-five-liter pack across Europe and the US Northwest, then found myself back in my old college town. This time I wasn't getting paid in National Park passes or per diems to cover backpacking meals, but a solid government paycheck. With the paycheck came the responsibility of being the lead ranger, which included a hefty ring of gate keys, a brick of a handheld radio that would cost me two grand if lost or damaged, and interns of my own, two outdoorsy college boys who looked older than me.

I had an assigned rig for the season, shared with the trail crew on my off days. It was a flatbed Chevy crew cab still boasting that classic Forest Service green paint job, a trend the agency has gradually phased out with stark white fleets. Beyond the allure of its good-old-days green, the truck wasn't good for much. Because it was a flatbed with only a small lock box where the chainsaw and chaps lived, my crew and I had to pile all of our personal and trail gear into the cab—full packs, handsaws and axes, maps and fliers, and a five-foot crosscut saw strung diagonally across the seats. The rig's fuel tank didn't trigger an automatic shutoff when filling up, and the suspension rattled to the point I was convinced the whole thing was falling to pieces below me.

On top of it all, the flatbed was a manual. I didn't know this until my first week on the job, not until I'd slid into the driver's seat and felt my hand fumble with air as it searched for the transition lever. I hadn't touched a stick shift since the Jeep, back in high school, and I felt all the elation and giddy freedom of the start of the season drain away. I'd pictured myself crawling up backroads to trailheads with one arm drifting out the open window, unencumbered by the technicalities of manual machinery, driving from town into the glacier-toned Rattlesnake Mountains with no challenge of the in-between. With all my elation about the old-fashioned perks of the job—the half-century-old crosscut saws and radio communication bounced off mountain repeaters and off-trail navigation with only a map and compass—I'd forgotten I didn't have the luxury of a rig that knew how to heave itself up a mountain.

There were few things in my life I'd given up on, and driving stick was one of them. I ambled back across the fleet parking lot and stood in the doorway of my supervisor's office.

"I forgot to mention something," I said in a voice that reminded me of a dog found rooting in garbage. "I don't know how to drive a manual." It didn't seem necessary to mention I'd already tried.

My boss didn't skip a beat. "We'll just have a lesson, then," he said. His clear-cut optimism, underlined by a toughness cultivated in the Marines, rarely waned, which surprised me, seeing how many years he'd worked in public land management. We walked back to the gated lot and got in the cab of the flatbed, and just like that I was back to practice drives.

While everyone from the office was home firing up grills for Memorial Day, I practiced. The Missoula Ranger District is part of the old Fort Missoula grounds, and I had no shortage of empty roads and gravel lots to patrol. I lurched around the fort in random circles, stop to first gear to second to stop over and over again. Sometimes I shifted easily all the way to fourth, and other times I staggered the flatbed so bad I made myself carsick. Still I made a semblance of progress. The Chevy, when it came down to it, wasn't the Jeep. And the Jeep had been a horrible rig.

When my interns came on in June, I still lurched and stalled out the truck. But they didn't say anything, and I learned to shrug off the mortification, or else pack it down somewhere out of sight. With all the other quirks of the flatbed coupled with other responsibilities—gear lists and itineraries and always changing weather—mastering the clutch stopped dominating my worries. It settled to a low simmer beside everything else.

There are three main access points to the Rattlesnake Wilderness, and the one we used most often follows a roadbed beside Rattlesnake Creek through the National Recreation Area to the wilderness boundary. Road 99 used to be the track white settlers had used decades before, likely a Salish route before that, and it snakes through cottonwood-shaded meadows and pockets of ponderosa pine and tamarack. Past mile eight the road climbs out of a thicket of firs and redcedar into a hairpin turn, treading beside old fire-scarred trunks of western larch. And then Road 99 leaves behind the comfort of solid ground and cuts straight through two abrupt talus slopes.

From the main trailhead to the wilderness boundary, it's the only stretch of the sixteen-mile track with exposure. Rocks the color of coral split onto the roadbed to nip at all-terrain tires, and the talus fields extend a good two hundred feet above and below the road. It's a sharp slope on the downhill side, nothing but sharp edges of granite and hodgepodge scree all the way to Rattlesnake Creek. There's one patch of the roadbed unhitched to the mountainside, a lip of loose rocks that sloughs downslope bit by bit every year.

The loose section of roadbed was never bad enough for structural concern, just enough to always tease the possibility of a sudden tumbling shudder. For all the superb views from that spot, I never got used to the slumped hollow, watched my knuckles turn white on the steering wheel. I kept plenty of pressure on second gear, coaxing the flatbed over the dip, which would shift ever so slightly every time. The rattle of lichen-rough rocks against each other vibrated up through the flatbed's poor suspension and into my knees and ribs.

Sometimes I peered out the window at the drop-off an arm's reach away. If the talus gave, we'd slide and roll and topple against all those molars of granite. In the half-unconscious blur of falling asleep, this is the feeling that seizes me awake again—not just a sense of falling, but stones shouldering against each other as I go, metal screeching to a stop in a watery crumple.

The roadbed never gave way, that summer or the following three that I stayed as lead wilderness ranger. As the season progressed, the shifty stretch of Road 99 turned from a literal bump in the road to a stand-in for all the anxieties damming up inside me—the constant transition between a human-flush world and a human-absent one, fits of bad weather, the way trail users always looked to my interns instead of me for authority. I'd spent the previous six months constantly in a new place—western Scotland, Budapest, central Oregon—and now I was patrolling tight circles in the same thirty-two thousand acres of wild country, about to jump off again towards Appalachia. There was a persistent dread in my throat, sharper than the axes my crew and I spent days sharpening, and it was rooted in a premature homesickness and a bad stretch of road just the same.

•

We pull away from the Laugarvatn hostel at five after nine. In the face of all the driving we've been doing, I take some advice from our guide and find some music to overlay with the landscape blurring past. Vigga had suggested Björk, which I don't have much of an understanding for, but I do have the album *My Head Is an Animal* from the Icelandic band Of Monsters and Men. I can place the sparsity of their lyrics with this unadorned topography—broad and wide and overwhelmingly treeless, so that any sense of scale I have is thrown out the window.

I've been trying to shed my habit of comparison, not see Iceland propped against other landscapes. Its golden hills and lack of single-trunked plants remind me of the Scottish highlands and inner Hebrides, and where we find snow my mind tugs back to Montana's Beartooth Mountains and snowfields domed over spills of runoff. The northern sunlight slants about the same as it does during Finnish Lapland's summer-long day.

I push all those places back into memory. We turn east into the Markarfljót River Valley, and the paved road drops to black gravel. To the south, furrows of waterfalls spill between black outcrops. Eyjafjallajökull rests heavy and polished against an equally unblemished blue sky. Iced tongues drape down the mountains like the whole glacier is gripping the black earth.

As the bus bumps deeper into the valley, I lose myself in the mountains and river channels with all their scars and scratches. We pass a few all-terrain Jeeps charging into the water, some backhoes scraping fords to prep for the summer tourist season when most people don't have a Jeep or high-riding tour bus. The energy of this place is all openness and wildness, and I'm finally feeling all of it, the black waters glittering beside the road and northern sun blushing my face.

I think about what it would be like to return with a tent and pack and ramble for days, weeks, months across the Markarfljót's arteries and the glacier's rocky clutch.

We spill out of the bus at Stakkholtsgjá, a vertical-wall canyon patched in carpets of emerald moss. Terns zigzag across the blue strip of sky. I take off my shoes to cross a stream and find I have no interest in putting them back on. The canyon floor isn't much of a silky path of sand; rough basalt has crumbled down from glacial erosion, and even the dark sandbars grit into my calluses. I pick my way across the stones and splash into the glossed stream, meander from canyon wall to canyon wall. Between the unyielding edges of stones and stab of glacial meltwater, my feet start to ache in earnest, but now that's the whole allure.

I don't forget the shift of those cool rocks against my toes. I haven't forgotten the waver of balance in similar bedrock above Rattlesnake Creek either, so when, later in the afternoon, the tour bus tips into the ford, it's not a far stretch at all to feel how those stones move. They thud together, settle deeper underwater, packing into the depressions and corners of each other. The bus's gears and engine groans against gravity-bound lean.

Months before Eyjafjallajökull erupted, people documented tremors rattling its core. Before scars of magma stitched open, before locals saw jets of lava and steam and ash-clogged streams breaking up the land, the mountain's eruption was a thing felt and not seen.

The volcano had erupted before. Floods clawed and scraped and gouged a network of arterial channels into the landscape, but after each disturbance the scars smoothed over. These old tracks are easy to forget, tucked out of sight under glacial palms, seas of wind-ruffled grass, the slow recovery of birchwood. Eyjafjallajökull traces the ridges and hollows of gravity's narrative, millimeter of ice by millimeter of ice, no matter if that ice is freezing or melting. Nature, I've learned, is a master at hiding the entropy that fuels it.

The moment after the bus pulls onto dry land, my panic breaks open like Eyjafjallajökull. I hunch deeper against the windowpane to hide anything visible, but really the bulk remains unseen. The familiar raw helplessness scours into old channels, and I'm at a loss as to why this fear runs so unencumbered through my body, what with the rest of my classmates back to chatting and laughing away again. I give up trying to see deeper faults in the thick of the flood. Like the flights grounded across Europe as Eyjafjallajökull's ash pours over the North Atlantic, I lock down my facilities.

It takes quite a few more runs alone into the forest to hear the dull shift of those rocks and follow that echo to loose talus on Road 99. To remember Omar's precision with the clutch and remember the panic-flushed moment I felt myself rolling into gravity before the Jeep's engine caught on the streets of my hometown. To realize why I latched my focus to Omar and Vigga and our professors instead of enjoying the thrill of the experience with my classmates—a familiar terrain of responsibility. Of course it wasn't the same, but it was familiar enough, how I've always preferred the weight of losing control over never having it in the first place.

The tour bus continues down the road, and the terrain softens. Brushy mountainsides and waterfalls slip past the windows. The river continues its charge beside us, lapping over basalt and spits of coarse black sand. Channels split and merge, lean apart, knot together again. I stare out the window and hold onto this single comfort, that gravity pulls waters from marbled glacier to foam-strewn sea regardless of how deep the glacier has gouged its path there.

The tires hit pavement again, rising into a smooth whir. Sunlight streams behind me now, and I see a white haze opening across the coast ahead. Freed from the tension of uneven ground, the bus's engine spins high in third gear. Omar eases into fourth, and we drive out of that flood-scarred valley, held in the earth's spin by the catch of gears beneath our feet.

10

Cracking the Window

I have too many stories that end a hand's reach from hypothermia, close enough to touch but never take hold. Desperate for birdsong, hungry for the pitched snap of burning wood. In my mouth the taste of rain and damp snow.

You ask me how I'm not cold. The truth is I am unless I'm running, unless I'm moving. I've taught myself to accept it as a state of being, a practice. It takes years out-of-doors, skin to the elements, morning after morning shivering out of a sleeping bag. I've practiced sub-zero the most, windchill so strong my eyelids freeze together. I chase it in running shoes, love how a blizzard turns the hills half a mile from my home into a wilderness, a risk howling in whiteout.

What I don't say is that this is the easy part of the practice. Cold air moves downhill; like any body, it bows to gravity, sinks with water into shadows. Step outside and there it is, weighing and waiting. Always outside. Not many people see the distinction.

The difficult part comes with the click of the bedroom door, the cold I learned to make. Here's the hardest practice I kept for far too long—sleep chilled and tremble that warmth into sheets. Sleep where the air is too cold for bare skin. Sleep, above all, alone.

•

Winter begins in late August 7,690 feet above sea level. Fragile crystals spur down from low clouds, pricking the lake's chopped surface. The wind is a howl through cliff bands.

I stand drenched with fingers wrinkled white and step through the scraggly krummholz—subalpine fir and spruce twisted by the basin's haphazard gusts—to touch fingertips to McLeod Lake. Highest lake in the Rattlesnake Wilderness, highest source of Rattlesnake Creek, two days to reach. For me, one day blinked in sunlight and panic, the next smeared in rainclouds and determination. An old logging road, wolf scat, single track lost to time and underbrush. The musk of mountain goats, taste of rain a hundred feet from swirling to snow.

Here's the thing about McLeod Lake. Save for this shadow of vegetation on its south shore, the basin rests bare, rocky and humming the color of sunset stucco. It boasts no forested greenery like the other lakes of the Rattlesnake, and today it offers no reflection. Only a deepest cold blue, the kind that tends towards azure in sunlight. And as far as I know, the lake has no true outlet.

I told myself at the beginning of my third season working as a wilderness ranger in the Rattlesnake, I would touch the headwaters of Rattlesnake Creek. Really it's an impossible commitment. The creek has no contained body of water it anchors to. It simply begins somewhere in the thick of old-growth firs, a crease of land no different to the east or to the west. McLeod Lake rests a third of a mile away, five hundred feet higher, unattached.

It's a strange sight on a topographic map, a pale blue lake ringed by contour lines with not a thread of a stream hooking it downslope. It's an even stranger sight on the ground, hands and knees across talus and thanking the goats for stomping safe passage up crumbling breaks, only to stumble onto the rim of a lake with no marshy corner, no backlog of bone-white driftwood, no tipping point between still water and stream. McLeod rests below a peak of the same name—the wilderness's highest—like palms scooped through sand to the water table. Like a crater on the moon. Like a foreign, forgotten body.

Across the lake is a band of snowpack left over from last winter. New flurries spill down in broken curtains, shredded white against the rock's amber horizons. I'm soaked through, and I know I should be getting back to my camp before the snow line drops. But I crouch lake-bound to dip iced fingers into iced water one more time. Today I name this wind-ripped surface a source, but of what, I can't really say.

The wind doesn't stop. I open my mouth and howl back.

•

When we start spending the night together, I wake up burning under the covers. My house, with its poor insulation and inefficient furnace and unannounced drafts, isn't so bad. But at your place, under the down comforter and flannel sheets, I roast. I wake up thirsty, clammy, flushed. My sinuses clamp up; breathing becomes one-sided and halting.

"I'm sorry," I whisper, tossing the comforter back, moving away.

"It's okay," you say, crisscrossing your fingers into mine. "You can crack the window."

•

People are often mistaken about the source of hypothermia. You get too cold, they say, which isn't totally wrong. But really what happens is the body can't keep warm, which is an important distinction. Trapped in a half-frozen pond or exposed to a wind scraped down from the Arctic, blood vessels constrict like tributaries fringed in ice come November, slowing blood flow. Here's where frostbite comes in—no heat to the extremities, the far reaches of those vessels, and the elements begin to take control. It's not that the outside temperature is cold enough to freeze fingers like they're breakfast sausages forgotten in the car overnight, just that the body doesn't have enough heat to spare. Warmth gets pulled with the blood to core organs—lungs, liver, heart. Muscles, tapping laws of friction and metabolism, start to shake.

Some bodies are better than others at keeping this balance, learning what stretches of muscle and tendon to sacrifice. Eventually, though, there's a point of no return. Blood holes up around the heart, and the body forgets to shiver. The brain sits chilled against its dome. Systems flip and disorient as if caught in a whiteout. The message of *cold cold cold seek warmth* gets lost, scrambled through nerves forgetting their purpose. *Warm warm warm*, the body hums.

Some people, past that turning point, will tear off their jackets and pants. They fall drowsy. Search and rescue eventually finds them at the end of a trail of clothes, bodies draped halfway into the open water of a stream, desperate to cool off.

It's not a bad way to go, I think guiltily. Pleasantly warm, nodding off to sleep, surrounded by water and white.

•

Winter was settling into the valley when we met. Walking back to our respective cars, you asked if I was a hugger. I am not, at least to most people. But I said sure. The night air was sharp and cold; we stepped away and stood with hands in pockets.

My car took a minute to warm up, and I shivered in the seat watching you walk away. I shook the whole drive home, to the point where I worried about the tremble of my foot on the gas pedal. That night I couldn't stop shaking. That whole first month I could not stop shaking.

•

The day before winter begins at McLeod Lake, I break down in unorthodox panic. My surroundings don't seem to spur it. Sunlight washes across willow-sweet meadows and open forest where white snags stand as the remnants of the Mineral-Primm Fire. Rattlesnake Creek babbles its same song below the trail. My pack is relatively light—no crosscut saw, food for only two nights, not even a single-bit ax. Still, alone on the tread, I trip to my knees. Hands to summer grass. Claw through my mind and iron-aching chest for a source of this panic. My mouth is dry, face like rain.

The weather is supposed to turn bad, I tell myself. A hunting group might later show up where I'm planning to camp, two men with an A-frame tent and great distain for the Forest Service. The bears are starting to get bold this time of year.

But nothing holds. Nothing explains this stark despair. At camp I slip on work gloves and pull thistle and pepperweed until the sun tilts into evening. I break one of my backcountry rules and put in my earbuds to replace birdsong with human voices. A cool breeze eases down the creek bed, and on it, I can smell moisture hanging among the high ridges of the wilderness, ready to drop that night.

Usually I leave one section of my tent's rainfly open at night, letting the near-freezing breeze sift through the mesh and brush across my face. Tonight, though, I zip the rainfly shut early. I wake to heavy darkness and rain on the nylon outside.

•

If the temperature rises above twenty-three degrees Fahrenheit in the winter, a moose will overheat. Her coat holds onto heat by trapping air, and her undercoat is thick and soft, outer layer made up of hollow hairs. In her long legs, arteries run parallel to veins, outlets and inlets side by side. Blood flowing outward warms that returning to her core, so that she uses less energy, wastes less warmth. When she breathes, air dwells in the large dome of her muzzle; it does not rush, sharp and sub-zero, into her wide lungs.

The moose's body is made for cold. Faced with Chinook winds, an early thaw, late-winter sun, her mind tells her *too warm warm warm*. She moves onto cooler slopes, north- and east-facing, saunters through shaded copses of fir or willows, stripping the limbs for food. She might forgo her vigilance for a quick moment, swivel her ears against her neck, lay down to roll herself in the cool snow.

In summer she follows water. There, reeds grow thick in murk and sedges bunch into islands. She stands belly deep, blinking against light sourced from sky and the lake dappled like quartz all around her.

She's an excellent swimmer. I've seen this once, and you tell me you have too—a moose diving into a lake, slim neck and domed head and long legs disappeared completely into that deep blue.

•

"Where do you go?" you ask me one afternoon, the two of us sitting on my bed. "I see it in your eyes sometimes," you say, "like you disappear for a moment."

I close my eyes and try to understand this impulse to drift, and drift away from you. I see a wall of evergreens, snow domed over a lake's surface. A camp in a meadow walled by firs, a trail petering off to the north.

"Don't worry," you say, squeezing my palm. "You always come back."

•

Once, in college, I left my window cracked open too long into autumn and it froze that way until late February. All winter the cold snaked in, chilled my bedroom below fifty come morning. Which was still much warmer than outside, and the basement apartment was otherwise well insulated, and my roommate and I preferred saving money on our heating bill, thermostat staying at sixty regardless. Every dark morning I shivered into my clothes for the day.

I could have climbed down into the windowsill and banged the window tight against its frame. I could have gone to bed with my door left open so the cold air didn't pool in the bedroom with nowhere to go. But I didn't. I let the chill in all night, layered my warmth in quilt and cotton, never let the cold out. Truth is I've never slept better than when the tip of my nose is cold to touch.

•

The night of winter solstice, we build a fire out back. You bring a bundle of pinewood from the store while I attempt to split a round of cottonwood I saw draped in a paper *FREE* sign before the snow fell. The wood is either spongy or frozen, so we add it sparingly to the cuts of pine.

The sky sparks clear and cold, embers from our fire snuffing out alongside the stars. The smoke drifts without direction, and for weeks our clothes will smell of campfire. *You know what smoke follows*, we say to each other, grinning.

Winter will soon swallow the raised fire pit in snow, crust the plastic Adirondack chairs up to their armrests. I will be standing at my kitchen sink in mid-March, washing dishes, when I first notice the metal rim emerge again, a perfect circle in the snow.

•

Mama & baby moose in the woods today! 2/26, a message handwritten on white paper taped to a trail sign three blocks from my house.

All February the wind blows and windchills keep below zero. Snow drifts across the front walk, and my roommates and I run out of places to put it. Chickadees, grosbeaks, and nuthatches put up residence in the neighbors' line of cedar brushes across the street, dart to the bird feeder hanging from our roof to scatter husks of sunflower seeds to brash squirrels below. You and I make egg scrambles and pancakes and sit at the dining room table watching them flit through the sharp wind. One afternoon a group of people claim to see a bobcat in the woods across the street. Rattlesnake Creek freezes over. The Clark Fork River freezes over.

From the kitchen window I watch elk herds move across Mount Jumbo, dropping south from the Rattlesnake where I listened to their bugles through the fall. They come almost like clockwork, at six every evening, to paw through wind-shaved patches of snow. One day the city closes the mountain due to high urban avalanche danger. It's exactly five years after one tumbled down a chute into my neighborhood, burying four people, including two children. One woman died, surrounded too long in that cold white.

Now the weather has pushed this cow moose and her calf into a landscape of gridded asphalt and barking dogs. The city closes a trail in Greenough Park, which means the pair have migrated further down from Pineview Park, past where my house sits across from Rattlesnake Creek. Maybe, I think, one cold night they walked right outside my bedroom window.

In the wilderness I'm about as respectful of mother moose as I am mother bears. Still, while coasting through the off-season on unemployment and late-morning runs, I watch for her and the calf in the riparian areas along the creek where she was first spotted. I peer at stabs of tracks in the deep snow, jump at dark-coated hikers. My breath plumes and crystalizes onto my eyelashes. I wouldn't mind seeing her at a safe distance, each in our element.

Residents wonder if this is the best place for the pair, if relocation would be a better option. One day she approaches a group of people, and people wonder further. But the Parks and Recreation Department reiterates their trail closures and mandatory dog leashing. In the single-digit temperatures, sedation isn't an option. The drugs released from a dart gun mean the animal's body can no longer sustain its own warmth.

"There's no way we could drag her out of the brush before she got hypothermic," states the game warden. "People have other places to go."

•

In the backcountry there are two sources of warmth—fire and body heat. Of all the ledges into hypothermia I've stood on, none happened in circumstances where a fire was possible. I've been soaked through every time, and so was any deadwood with the potential to burn. I had no choice but to take the most self-sufficient option, returned to my tent to lay for hours in a dry sleeping bag, wearing all my wet clothes. They have to dry out somehow.

If someone turns hypothermic, they can't shiver themselves warm. They can't think properly, or coordinate their movements, or warm up in a sleeping bag even if they're dry. They have to find an outside source of warmth. A fire might work if the conditions are right. But the surest way, sometimes the last resort, is another body.

First aid courses have taught me this—crowd into a sleeping bag with the person, radiate your own body heat against them and the insulated down of the bag. The key is bringing their internal temperature back into a range where maybe, maybe, their circulation system will kick back into gear, remember the vessels of its flow.

I've never been in a situation that warrants this technique for myself or anyone else. But I've been close, felt that sleepy draw overcome the impulse to keep moving. It's an old habit, finding comfort in cold. An old practice to hole up around myself, name a source that doesn't come from anywhere or anyone else.

•

When I first started patrolling the Rattlesnake, having skipped working on a trail crew with tools named for their European wielders, I pronounced McLeod like it ended in *load*. That was wrong, I learned my second season. It tips off the tongue like *cloud*.

•

Winter ends in mid-March 3,192 feet above sea level. A final hard snow strips definition from the Clark Fork, smothering the air in white. We stand overlooking a single patch of open water. Ice caps the rest of the river, great plates three or four feet thick that jut and spur against each other.

Here it is again, the nameless despair. I love snowfall as much as the backcountry, but sometimes they don't hold me up. Sometimes this happens, just as it did at the sunlit camp three off-trail miles from Rattlesnake Creek's final source—paralysis, face like downpour, a terror I cannot trace. Snow plasters us, nests atop your hair. It's warm snowfall, too. I feel it soaking through my collar but I can't bring myself to move.

"I'm sorry," I say, and you shake your head.

"I don't want you to see this side of me," I add, which is also a quiet admission to myself that this is a side of me, no matter how much I try to outrun it. Some years are harder than others—chest pain a constant through my early twenties, friendships and family relationships stretched because I could not contain nor name what roiled inside me. Three therapists, one summer solstice afternoon where my thumb hovered over the call button to check myself into the hospital.

"What's a favorite river memory?" you ask.

I pitch my hands over my mouth and shake my head. "I can't," I manage. The truth is I can only stare at the gap of open water below us, slick and dark, and skirt away from the part of me that wants to disappear under the ice. I almost tell you this.

"That's okay," you say. Your hand circles the peaks of my back. The snow keeps coming down, melting against our warmth, soaking us through.

•

Hypothermia isn't entirely dependent on temperature. It's really anything that happens after the body's temperature drops below around ninety-five degrees Fahrenheit. "You can get hypothermic in seventy degrees," a boss once told me. "If someone can't keep themself warm, it doesn't matter if it's a balmy afternoon. An internal temp dropping to seventy will kill them."

Hypothermia above freezing temperatures isn't likely to occur outside of another trigger, which is often shock. A concussion might do it, a broken bone, sudden blood loss. I learned this in first aid class too—if someone goes into shock, regardless of the injury or conditions, wrap them up tight. Find heat—a fire, a bottle full of hot water, your own drumming heart. Faced with trauma, no matter how minor or reparable, staying warm is one of the first things the body forgets.

•

I call a friend who lives in the desert southwest. "I feel like all the sadness in the world is inside me," I say as snow cocoons the windows of my car. I tell her I don't know what has caused this, the animal sounds echoing in my mouth as I sit motionless in a dark parking lot. I'm not in shock. There's no hard line of trauma I can trace.

"I've been there a hundred times," she says. "Sometimes there's no one thing."

I confess to her that I'm afraid these shadows will cause me to lose you. That the part of me drawn to dark water will also send me sprinting away. I tell her of this harsh winter, how every sub-zero morning I ran into the wind, everything frozen and cold and white except for the blood pumping through my body. The two of us share this impulse of extremes, except hers is the opposite—she's a desert soul, rambling red rocks as the temperature spikes into triple digits. Neither of us can imagine how the other does it, but we understand why.

It stops snowing, squall bumping downriver, leaving the sky a starless navy black.

"To be completely honest," my friend says with a small laugh, "I'm a bit envious of you. I haven't broken down in a long time. Haven't been able to cry. We're so conditioned into holding back too much. It has to go somewhere eventually."

I think of this final full snow, the rivers and creeks still held up in ice. I think of the desert where she is, heavy orange sun and quiet cacti and dry rattle of spiny bushes. Water a variable, something to ration, something always fluid or a hallucination. Hills fissured in slot canyons, sparked by creosote in bloom. I try to imagine the dry desert air that smells of sunset and cool sand where it meets the water table. Try to take in this parched air instead.

My friend pauses, lets out a small breath as if she's turned to look out the window. "It's raining here," she says.

•

The cow moose and calf, likely following the riparian buffer of Rattlesnake Creek, make their way toward downtown one bluebird sky morning. They relax in the shallow snow, browsing on urban shrubs and lounging on front lawns. Police close off East Pine Street as the pair aim for the post office, the art museum, the rainbow crosswalk at Pine and Pattee. It's warm today, well into the upper twenties. The Department of Fish, Wildlife and Parks makes the call, and the cow and calf are tranquilized. They bed down between two homes, side-by-side and sleepy.

We drive by to see if we can catch the end of the excitement. We'd respect the yellow tape, of course, and especially the moose's space, but it's just hard to pass up. The sunshine falls through bare branches as welcome as warm honey.

By the time we turn onto East Pine, though, the drowsy cow and calf have been hauled off. All we find is a Department of Fish, Wildlife and Parks truck parked front bumper to front bumper with another pickup, jumper cables draped between them, battery cold.

•

The route up to McLeod Lake leaves the hollow of Rattlesnake Creek and breaks onto a ridge that burned in 2003. Or at least this is the route I take, one scoped from topographic maps and satellite images in the office beforehand. It's slightly less direct, curving north towards the northern edge of the wilderness, but I'd rather cover more open ground than head straight through dense underbrush where rainwater jumps against my limbs.

The rain sways across low ridges, uncommitted between drizzle and fog. Where the tree line breaks into the old burn, I smell damp willow and grouse whortleberry and creeping Oregon grape. Snags stand half-mast, white until the black-pointed tips where they snapped in licks of flame. Mirroring Rattlesnake Creek, this is the farthest reach of the Mineral-Primm Fire, an arm that barreled west into the basin before swinging north again and sputtering out.

Fire, unlike water, prefers moving uphill. While cold air sinks, warm thermals are coaxed higher by the flames, drying out the terrain above. Butterscotch pine needles bronze and curl to black. Green shoots of grass singe and crumple. It comes down to distance, too, a short step up for a flame already reaching skyward.

But fire's upward draw doesn't explain the Mineral-Primm Fire. The blaze started at least ten air miles to the southeast in harvested timberland, swallowing the Rattlesnake Wilderness's entire east flank as it climbed the gradual slopes. But then, riding the ridge towards Triangle Peak, it spun west and dropped into the basin of upper Rattlesnake Creek, tumbling 1,500 feet in less than two miles. It swung northwest again, stretched like morning cat, wove up the rocky spines fanning down from McLeod Lake.

I don't know the bodies of fire like I do water. Then again, you remind me, just as my friend in the desert does, I am a fire sign, born surrounded by winter and mountains. But I like to believe the fire burned with a familiar hunger—to touch the source of something loved, to chase a contrast and dive in the space between.

I pause in the open stretch of burned forest. Small gullies wrinkle down the slope. They cup harebells and bluebells already bloomed, slump with damp earth. Water spills between stucco stones. This late in the season, any one of these channels could be the first flow of Rattlesnake Creek. Any one could be the smallest liquid body, a skiff of snow tipped damp.

But the flames stopped, I remind myself. The Mineral-Primm Fire never reached McLeod Lake, sputtered out even before walls of talus and chalky breaks. When I press on again, climbing into winter's first snowfall, I leave the fire scar behind. Leave the shadow of its heat like a question, push on to reach what flames couldn't. Water dapples my eyelashes, soaks into the soft leather of my boots, finds its way through my clothes to fan across my skin.

The point, I realize, isn't finality. The point, against all the hard lines of water on my map, is that there is no point of no return.

•

Here's a favorite river memory. The day after spring equinox, I put on my Chacos for the first time in half a year and walk downtown, below Madison Street Bridge where willows streak amber across snowbanks. The river opened up three days ago. Navy black water shushes past tables of ice still impressively thick. The crystals jab and melt against my bare feet as I posthole down to the river's edge.

Rattlesnake Creek meets the Clark Fork here, a commonplace confluence between the Hilton Double Tree and low-roofed houses off East Front Street. Its older and deeper name, given by the Salish, is Nłʔaycčstm—place of the small bull trout. While floating on inner tubes during the summer months, it's easy to miss if not for the sudden shadow of cold water, the snowmelt and runoff from chilled lakes I've spent my summers patrolling. I clamber over ice jams to this meeting point. The cold water spills across round stones, marbling reflections like stained glass.

My feet don't smart anymore but simply glare red and flushed in the creek water. Which is also the river water, I realize, also snow from this endless winter, also ice from last winter. And, I remember, also water from the highest waters of McLeod Lake, where I stood seven months ago, drenched and cold and alone.

In that wilderness I turned focus to a different practice, the mottled line between solitude and isolation. Not many see the distinction. Especially those who seek one and only tumble, weeping, into the other. It's not about one highest origin, one farthest source, one welcome warmth. I learned to listen to those bodies—iced and cuffed in air and as sunset blue as your eyes. I practiced listening to my own. Translate *This is what makes me feel alive* to simply *I am alive.* Translate loads into clouds that lift moisture beyond our reach.

At the confluence of Rattlesnake Creek and the Clark Fork, I stop to stack stones, each lighter than the one at its base. I've never done this before, preferred to leave my impermanent mark through prints of my limbs in the snow. The rocks wobble, turn against each other. Their masses don't matter much—it's all about contact, the points of balance where one will hold the other upright. I take the time, feet long ago gone numb, to find the places where one subtle ledge can rest in a delicate depression of another.

•

That night I stretch out of sleep hot and thirsty. To reach my water bottle, I bend with an unnecessary grace over you, pause in the dark to consider opening my lips to the soft peak of your shoulder. So often the moonlight tips over Mount Jumbo, turning the hillside bone white outside my window, catching your face in a way more akin to firelight. So often when we're falling asleep, your breath turns deep like a surf against cool sand.

But the space below me is empty. I remember you're not staying over tonight, that I'm sleeping alone, that my skin flushes hot regardless. I find my water and drink slowly, parched with three a.m. thirst, until I can hear the water spilling into the basin of my belly. Sometimes, I remind myself, I can feel my heartbeat there too, an echo through water, a grounding absent of earth.

In the morning I will wake to the sound of Rattlesnake Creek washing its banks for the first time since autumn. Even through my shut window, I will hear the ice's absence as currents stumble downslope, a backdrop to robins and geese singing of open water.

Here's a metaphor I've never been able to figure out—the land a body, water blood. I read maps the same way I read books, and this is their endless story—watersheds run like branches, like roots, like lungs, like capillaries. But in bodies like ours direction is fluid, cold blood returning from fingertips and callused soles, warm blood drumming through four silky rooms. Veins and arteries braid in the dark, the most important currents tucked against bone. They are unmoved by gravity, contained within a vessel that is.

I'll tell you where I go when my eyes are closed or clouded—the rutted path that runs parallel to Rattlesnake Creek, all the way to its highest shore, chasing a question as cyclical as springtime. I can't decide if the heart is a sea, or it's the quiet clap of moose hooves on an alpine lake, whether a source is the hollow where all that heaviness pools, or the place where we begin.

11

Reasons to Carry Bear Spray

1.

The man with dead grouse piled in the bed of his pickup will call you brave. Do not interpret this as anything but what it is, which is a threat. "You know there's grizzlies in this area, don't you?" he will say. "Brave of you to be up here alone."

Be cordial. Say thank you. Bury the anger in your voice only deep enough so that you'll be able to dig it up later. Don't let him find it. Give him only the satisfaction of your stuttering tongue. He will twist your yielding like a grouse's neck and think his muscled wrists strong. Let him.

He wants you to be angry. That's why—when the two of you met on the trail, you pulling slash across a tread that shouldn't be there, him rattling down on a mountain bike with a hunting bow strapped to his broad back—he immediately pulled his phone out and began recording. "You leftist environmental extremists are infiltrating the government," he said. "Locking up these lands. You want it all for yourself."

He wants you to be afraid. He asks for your name and, because you already have a nameplate pinned to your uniform front, you give it to him. Don't think about the fear rippling like broken thunder inside your chest. Continue to call him sir.

Remember the canister of bear spray clipped to your side, swinging against your right hip, but how could you think of anything else since the moment he skidded pale grains of quartz against your boots, twisted his face into fury, and spat, "What the fuck?" As you walk a quarter of a mile back down the trail with him right beside you—berating you, arguing with you, recording you— don't think about what killed the grouse in his truck bed, how your back is now turned to an armed, angry man.

Do step back into your Forest Service rig. Do remember that the man's truck is parked facing a shut gate. He will have to turn around. This will give you a few minutes to drive ahead, for the dust to settle back into the washboards and the trace of you to be gone. Remember you know this place better than him. Remember when he said there weren't any goddamn elk in this country and you replied you'd seen plenty of droppings and tracks just that morning. Remember when he scoffed that it was nearly impossible to reach Bull Lake and you told him you'd made it there twice this summer. Remember how his eyes looked like he was falling.

Start the engine and drive away without looking back. Do not think about the fist thrumming with hot blood around your throat. Drive, but don't continue down the way you came, the only way out. Turn onto a side road, a dead-end road. Stop in front of a locked gate, draw your trembling legs from the cab, and unlock the gate. Don't think about the irony. Drive through and lock it behind you. Keep driving until a bend in the hillside hides you, until it's just you and the warm truck and a carpet of knapweed across the roadbed and wind brushing through alder above you. Until, again, you're alone.

As is protocol, pull out your satellite phone and listen to the signal ping through the atmosphere to whatever vessels sweep, invisible and latched to sunlight, overhead. Call the Forest law enforcement officer first, then your supervisor, to relay what happened. You can come back early, use sick leave, stay home and write up the incident report from your back porch and spend the evening watching a movie about eight women who plan a jewelry heist and get away with it.

First, though, you can falter. Bend towards the dry ground and heave all the broken words from your lips. Do not blame yourself. Do not think about all the shut gates with ramshackle pickups parked in front of them. There's no need to feel guilty for hiding behind gates only you have the keys to. Keep some things for yourself.

Think of the quiet bodies of the grouse. Remember they can only fly as high as branches, never to the sky. Grouse can't soar. Their plumage is just a puffed-out buffer against falling. Remember that their only defense is to rush what frightens them.

2.

Don't call yourself lucky. Luck is for pinochle and traffic lights and good roommates on Craigslist and the knot of bad weather that breaks the minute you step onto the trail. When you read story after story of sexual harassment in the Forest Service and Park Service and interagency fire crews, don't say it surprises you. It doesn't, even though it hasn't happened to you. Do not call this shelter of trauma luck. Luck pardons those who would harm you. Luck turns your hands either passive or at fault.

When you attend a training about standing up to workplace harassment, bury your anger again. You are told of the long, bureaucratic process it takes for a complaint to bounce around HR up to Washington and back to the local office, where the details of punishment are confidential. The person in question may simply be moved out of a leadership role, put in a different duty location. Sure, they will be punished. But you, or anyone else, probably won't know how. This is to protect the harasser. Do not question this logic.

Do not think too much about the extra weight of protocol. Field evacuation forms for splintered bones and hypothermia, certifications for the chainsaw and crosscut. Practice the release of bear spray in an empty field prickled in tumbleweed. Add the thought of leap-frogging line officers to make a complaint, rating the severity of the harassment, parsing which HR call center is applicable, launching shock into nondisclosure agreements. Do not think too much about this added layer of awareness, an inversion of smoke atop haze. Keep your eyes open for mountain lions, handguns strapped to hips, hazard trees, meth labs, bears, militia logos on tailgates, game cameras, bull moose, darkening skies. Add an unfamiliar trail or fire crew. Add a shared bunkhouse. Add an office.

Tell yourself this meeting is still progress. Remember there are middle-aged men in the group. They have daughters. Their fury is valid and it will carry more weight than yours. Do not question this, not right now. Slip your thumbnail under the clip of your pen and concentrate on the slim nudge of force it would take to snap it across the conference room. Study the white creases in the plastic, beading there like graupel. Think about the millimeters your thumb has to go before the clip breaks. Do not break it. Not yet.

Luck is for huckleberry hunting and which radio repeaters will catch over cliff bands. For days off that happen to fall when Brandi Carlile comes to town and trees toppling just shy of the tread. For raffle tickets and online dating and winning three hundred bucks at the slot machines. For the doe skirting into the ditch at the last moment. The rest you build with intention. The rest is shaped and tacked and plastered by blistered palms into a ladder still for the taking. Some days the ladder lifts your confidence. Some days it reveals only your vulnerability.

Let your forearms ache with the weight of an ax. Remember how you feel when you carry your tools from your rig into the shop, heavy across your shoulders. Inside, splash a whetstone with cool water, trace it in soft circles over the blade. Shave the metal down to its finest ridge. This is where the power waits, millimeters from nothing. Run your thumb over top, protected by the callus you've worn there, tender to the finest lip that will gut deadwood roots.

3.

When the clerk at the running store tells you this canister of pepper spray is best for close range, nod your head. You've started running alone miles and miles back into Pattee Canyon, where you hear of black bears loping alongside joggers and mountain lions stalking kids at the bus stop. Tell the man you're not too worried, that a small canister should be fine. Only mention the lions and bears. But mostly, remember the story you heard of a woman running the riverside path at dusk. Remember why you need close-range pepper spray.

If it's dark, carry this canister almost everywhere with you. When you walk home from campus, past the frat houses with their thumping basses and drawn blinds, cross to the opposite sidewalk and coax the canister into your palm. Nudge it in your shoulder bag when you go out, even though it's a pain to rifle around to reach your wallet. Do not let it settle to the bottom of the bag among crinkled receipts and grocery lists on Post-it notes and loose change dragging on your shoulder like an anchor.

When you move across the country for grad school, bring the small canister with you. Leave it in your school backpack for walking home after evening classes, and when your friend tells you she saw a man jerking off into the bushes blocks from your apartment one night, transfer it back to your pocket.

For a year your room will face the fire escape, and a skinny man with his hood drawn will sit on the stairs late into the night outside your window. Switch the alarm on the windowpane, draw your blinds, pin a blanket across the whole windowsill. Hook the pepper spray—the bear spray for close encounters—on your lamp, right by your head. Call the property management company. Tell them the motion-sensor cameras on the fire escape aren't working. Check the lock to the door that opens to the landing. When you see the skinny man tucked into the corner against the door one night, pour half a refill bottle of liquid soap on the step in the morning. Bang on the door before you go to bed, watch for his shadow to steal away. Check the deadbolt every night.

Count the days until you return home, where you can tell yourself the pepper spray is for curious bears and lions perched in ponderosa limbs. Lying in your bed, learn to count your heartbeats, until they patter beyond number and roar like a spring flood in your mouth.

4.

The bear's prints are twice as wide as your palm. In the grainy spring snow, press your fingertips into the depressions pushed in by the toes. Claws made for grubbing curve into the drift. Think about what it would mean to greet this bear's warm paws.

Follow the stride down into a gully, back up a cutbank. Do not stray too far; this is your first work patrol of the season, slogging atop five-feet drifts, and there is no trail. You haven't been up this way in two years.

Remember the curve of Lake Creek below, rushing past meadows clouded by beargrass come August. Remember the slope of the land, snowpack or not. You have been here before. You have coaxed trailside huckleberries into these same palms, pitched fallen snags downslope. You know where you're headed.

Remember the hunger of the bear, the lunch chilled in your pack. Remember this presence, solitude, humility. You are not afraid.

Remember this feeling. Like the treetops will buoy you into sky, like the land is the language you know best. Like danger holds no ill intent, only a sky that will drop squalls across your shoulders, only a bear as curious and wild as you.

5.

When headlights swallow moonlight from the dome of your tent, cut your sleep-heavy conversation to silence. You and your friend, lying here in your sleeping bags, can talk about your love lives later. Listen to the rumble of an old engine in the pullout where you are car camping, growl of exhaust over dry-packed dust. Listen to the vehicle roll back and forth as if it's turning around but doesn't. Look at your friend through the grainy orange light. The engine chokes to silence.

Slowly unzip one of the mesh windows of the tent, then the fly. Watch a man slide from the ramshackle SUV, walk around the vehicle. He doesn't seem to notice your car is also parked in the pullout. He doesn't seem to notice your tent is pitched a couple dozen yards away, but you never know. The high-beams did catch your shadow.

Watch the man unload objects from the bed, drop them lightly on the hard dusty ground. Some make a quiet thump, buffered with air, but none catch the faint light from the man's cab. Wonder what he's doing. Give him the benefit of the doubt, until you feel your friend stiffen beside you, her breaths quiet but loaded with fear.

Listen to the creek just down the field whisper its words through the night. Do not move, but watch, still as a whitetail before she bolts. The man's hands knot together and scratch a flame into the darkness, which he drops on the pile at his feet.

"Oh, no he's not," you hiss. For a moment, let yourself think of fire restrictions and tinder-dry grass in this meadow and the jackstraws of fallen lodgepole sprawling these mountains. Do not trip into guilt for taking yourself, briefly, away from your own danger. Let your mind babble upstream, thread into the landscape, break the brittle twigs of kinnikinnick. Here it is dry. Here the land will buck with flames.

Your friend whispers your name. Pull your mind back from the brittle tongues of cheatgrass. Watch the man. Watch how the firelight, worming through stacks of floppy paper, dims and catches his sharp cheekbones. He circles back around his vehicle. The cab light switches dark.

"Nope, we're going now," your friend says. You hesitate only briefly. Then you do go. In the quick sprint from the tent to your car, take only what your hands can hold—phone, keys, and the canister of bear spray. Sprigs of hollow grass stab bare feet. Moon-cool air rushes against your faces, and then you are there, heartbeats thundering into eardrums. Click the car doors locked.

But your hands hesitate with the keys. Look to your friend, the moonlight like milk on her face, behind you where the man hangs in the shadow of his SUV, back to the silhouette of your tent in the field. "We need to go," she says again. Forget the fire, the restrictions. Remember where you are. Remember who you are.

Your friend repeats your name, a spark of recognition where your mind swarms for excuses. "This is your life," she says.

And you look again at the black dome of your tent. "I know," you murmur, but you are thinking of everything left there in the grass—tent and sleeping bag and your grandfather's Leatherman and rain jacket and maps and field journal where you've scribbled your soul wild. "I know," you say. But really you mean all these things are your life; what you bear in the backcountry presses heavy against your spine, keeping you warm and dry and fed and comfortable and comforted and hydrated and free, as if with every ounce of gear gained your body sheds what the world deems it—vulnerable, fragile, passive. Here are the objects you carry to make yourself feel less like one. Here are the buffers that unwind a narrative your hands won't let go—that out here, moonstruck under nylon, all you should fear are bears.

Turn to your friend. Learn to accept when it is time to go. Jam the keys in the ignition. Shift briefly into reverse, spray the dogwoods trimming the creek with blood-red light, then spin around the pullout. Press your bare foot onto the gas pedal down the dirt road, following the moon. You and your friend shudder out breaths; let your strong hand find hers. Leave everything else behind.

12

The Long View

I. Heart

Sickness works like this. There is something foreign in the body. A virus, a bloom of bacteria, havoc of single-celled organisms in the gut. The immune system blitzes what is unwanted—cells suffocating others that shouldn't be there, purging the respiratory or digestive systems, amping up a fever to shatter a virus to bits. You feel sluggish, drained, exhausted. Then the body rids itself of the unwanted, or medicine pitches in. You get better, or you die. Don't forget this part, the binary we're taught of disease.

Autoimmunity works like this. There is no foreign attack. There is no external threat. There is only DNA gone askew, the body tripped up, attacking itself, fatigue of a fight without truce. Confusion, antibodies spilling into the bloodstream. A body forgetting it belongs to itself.

If my breastbone were an alpine table, this all would have started cupped in the ridges of my ribs, those soft basins heavy with bad water. Something went wrong in the bedrock—could be the Swedish heritage, could be the Basque. Maybe there are tailings wedged in the talus, leeching bitterness the color of a favorite sunset.

This is how my body feels, an ecosystem misreading itself, rooted back to exhaustion and granite pressure. I'd place the first sighting, that pinpoint on a map, beside my heart, the dome over my lungs. Name it solid, constant. Name it a tiredness that holds me down when I want to run. Name it by feel, by years of knowing something is off. The pressure tightens across my breastbone. When I breathe in, it strikes like lightning.

•

I'll tell you a secret. I'm afraid of nature right now. Not of bears or tumbles from cliffs, not of windstorms or mountain lions or wildfires scorching trees to matchsticks. I'm afraid of the looming unknown that has nothing to do with exploration or discovery. I'm afraid of the mess.

•

Of course we'll start with glaciers. They're melting. You know this.

At the end of the last ice age, glaciers sauntered back north, exposing mountain ranges they'd gnawed to hills and marshy basins. These lowlands seeped full of meltwater, forming today's Great Lakes. If you drive far west from this region, the first snowcapped mountains to thrust up from the plains are the Beartooths. Most people, weary from the flatness of the Dakotas, promised Rocky Mountain majesty, stumble from RVs to watch shaggy goats from the roadside. Snow fields drip near year round, faster and faster these days.

Glacier National Park gets most of the press for glaciers in the lower forty-eight. Glacier just won't be Glacier without glaciers, people say, weighing the loss of a namesake as much as the great slabs of ice themselves. But the Beartooth Mountains have glaciers tucked against their flanks as well. There are hundreds, both cirque and rock glaciers, more than Glacier National Park. Of all the glaciers in the Northern Rockies, the Beartooth Range holds fifteen percent of them.

I wish I could say I'd touched one of those melting bodies like I have in Glacier National Park. From a distance, sure. My dad and I scattered our family dog's ashes with a smear of peanut butter in the long and bare valley below Sky Top Glacier, watching wild geraniums flash in the wind of an approaching storm. One morning I saw the biggest black bear of my life between slats of lodgepole beside Silver Lake, which is fed off Grasshopper Glacier, both of us with nothing on our backs but the gray magic before dawn. According to one study, Grasshopper Glacier lost something like half its area and ninety percent of its volume in less than a century.

The Beartooths' largest glacier is Castle Rock Glacier, curled on the plateau far away from threading trails. It's taken to the high country like a wolverine, with jaws that break stone and an aversion to being seen by anyone except higher peaks. But it's starving fast. Between 1952 and 2003 the glacier shed sixty meters of thickness. That's over an arm-span's worth every year. That's the closest I ever want to be to a bear.

Glaciers are defined by density, not age. The longer a tongue of snowpack sits in a cirque, the more it settles on itself, forming sandpaper horizons just like soil. Snowfields that aren't quite dense enough to be called glaciers can still be hundreds or thousands of years old, and there are even more of these in the Beartooths, many unnamed, sprawling, and dripping thin. Come summer, their meltwater follows tourists back east, slipping at ease with elevation, onto the Great Plains to dampen corn and soybeans and wheat, and more often to join ceaseless April rain and drown them.

Up on the Beartooth Plateau, scientists walk across earth pressed down like an animal had bedded there. Glacier lilies knit the slope, stretching into this uncapped ground for the first time in hundreds of years. You know the story. The ice is going, going, gone.

II. Eyes

Below the plateau, in the dry timber, someone flicks a cigarette butt onto a cut slope matted with cheatgrass, or dry lightning tongues a hollow snag. The lodgepoles catch with a disturbing hunger. The air is saccharine with huckleberries and disease.

•

On a clear day the view from the top of Lolo Peak, leaning over the Missoula Valley, extends nearly forty-five miles in each direction. That's over six thousand square miles of vista, a dozen mountain ranges, valley bottoms wrinkled with generations of snowmelt. In summer, fires burn in the peaks in and around Glacier National Park, smudging the view to the northeast like someone has swiped their thumb down the ragged backbone of the Missions. I've shed the belief that nature is a blanket healer, but somewhere in that shift I told myself distance would do the trick. I've never stopped peering toward the most distant thread of horizon.

Maybe I smelled the smoke then. Maybe that smudge found its way into the rim of my eyes too, and I took it for altitude or strain from too long focusing on my boots on rough talus. I'm better at the long view. How the mountain spoons its north summit, trips like a corduroy skirt all the way down to the golden cottonwood valley. Never mind the sting of tears; the view up here is just that good. Never mind the smudged glass, two pictures millimeters from aligning, like those songs where the singer layers their own voice a quarter second behind. The pieces don't quite meet. They never do anymore, but I only notice if I'm looking for everything to make sense.

•

In July of 2017 a glint of lightning finds dry pines and takes to Lolo Peak. The fire begins about a mile west of the summit, and from there continues to sweep across ridges, wrapping around the mountain in a shawl of flame. Winds gust, shift, sweep embers high into the copper sky. The cinders land on the next bluff over, tearing into fir and lodgepole and old giants of whitebark pine. The fire swarms higher, higher upslope, lapping into columned stands of subalpine larch.

Flames reverse, spin and tumble downslope. On its eastern side the fire eyes the Bitterroot River and closes the highway, and on its southern flank it paces the edges of Lolo Creek. Pilot cars lead traffic into the walls of smoke, high beams dimmed to a child's nightlight, the whole surrounding world shut in sepia.

Two homes burn down in the fire. Three thousand people are evacuated, told to grab what they can and leave. Sheriff's deputies weave up ponderosa-pillared drives, knock on front doors until someone opens. They have to leave. This is no disaster to wait out.

There's no easy answer when it comes to wildfire in the West. Remember, nature is messy. Nature feeds on entropy, continual chaos, disturbances like wind and flame and flood to stack baselines back into an ecosystem. Lodgepole pine have serotinous cones sealed in resin that will only open after the parent has burned to a charcoal skeleton. Larch layer bark thick enough to insulate their living rings from flames, all while depending on the fire to scorch a clean slate for seedlings below. Slopes are charred to black dust one year, then splashed with willow and fireweed and alder the next. Elk herds flock and grow fat on the green.

Which is to say there's no one reason the Lolo Peak Fire sprawled across almost fifty-four thousand acres, consumed three homes, took one human life—a firefighter trying to beat back the spread. The whitebark pines have held their branches high for hundreds of years, waiting for that lightning strike. The subalpine larch kept their tough skins. The lodgepole pine crowded thick above self-pruning Doug firs. Some of their cones opened to a dim understory; some stayed closed like a wax seal on a love letter. Decade by decade, small fires were put out. The fuel load grew and grew.

We learn that fire is bad. We learn that trees are timber, a product grown and harvested under the Department of Agriculture. We learn a black bear cub stumbled onto a fire line in New Mexico with blistered paws. We learn to protect forests without listening to the whitebark, the lodgepole, the longleaf pine, the black-backed woodpeckers. We learn we're not as powerful as we think, so we turn the other way, build another watchtower.

•

My rheumatologist recommends starting hydroxychloroquine. My diagnosis is still a working diagnosis, she says, but the drug should help. The fatigue will lessen, she tells me. The muscle weakness, chest tightness, lightheadedness. Brain fog lifting like the morning after a rainstorm, the kind that scrubs the forest floor of needles.

Somewhere in my vessels and lobes and lymphocytes, there's a rankled lie. The main theory of autoimmunity goes that the immune system catches wind of a foreign threat, attacking whatever it first comes across—a hip joint, a kidney, tattered collagen. The body is exhausted because it is fighting. The body is exhausted because it's being attacked. The catch is that it's all the same energy source, one ecosystem caught in chaos.

Hydroxychloroquine works by scrambling the narrative of self-destruction among immune system cells, clamping what's gone haywire. Scientists don't know exactly how or why, since the drug was originally created as an antimalarial with a later bonus of slowing progression of systemic autoimmune diseases. Instead of a clamp, though, I see a curtain. I want the hundred-mile view to sift sense from static. You can't unravel a why without its echo, but then again, I'm running out of sick days, and I'd like to keep my kidneys.

The drug carries its side effects and risks double-fold: gastrointestinal distress in the short term, chance of cardiomyopathy and retina damage in the long term. I go to the optometrist with a Post-it note of names tight in my palm—visual field test, fundus autofluorescence imaging, spectral domain optical coherence, multifocal electroretinogram. In the visual field test, small dots light up a dome like a bleary sun through wildfire smoke.

Autoimmune diseases are variable and chronic. They are a fire on the horizon and a fire at your feet. I take the words my doctor gave me and stare at the view ahead—maybe kidney failure, maybe myositis, maybe pericarditis, maybe pleurisy, maybe cancer. Maybe remission or stability; there's a good chance of that since we caught it early, after all. Or maybe blindness from the medication. One maybe at the expense of another, or maybe, in a slow and bluebird spin atop some rocky peak where lodgepole knot their pitch-kissed cones below, there are too many maybes, and the horizon smudges regardless.

III. Blood

When I check into my rheumatology clinic, a receptionist hands me a clipboard stacked with papers instructing me to check off how severe my pain is and how difficult it is to tie my shoes. There's a poorly photocopied sketch of a skeleton, hands and feet blown out of proportion so it's easy to circle individual digits and tarsals.

This is the beauty my dad taught me of maps—one point here, and here, and nowhere else. I think of the Continental Divide ambling west of my hometown of Helena, MacDonald Pass in the heart of winter, only a half dozen lodgepole dimmed to rusty needles. Back then the pain was probably toes dipped in frostbite. I remember it like fire, and I remember the ease of localizing it, a numbness then hot iron clamped around my toes and nowhere else. Beyond that place, a white and moldable world domed in the bluest blue. Pines stacked their shadows as far as I could see, so what was one more toe throbbing like a coyote's cry in the back woods?

Now the points are clear, angry red welts on my fingers and toes. One winter night, the brush of sheets is too much. Toes swell to cherry tomatoes, throb angry and razor stiff. I hobble to the freezer for the release of frozen peas even though I figure cold won't help in the long run. Stagger on my partner's arm even though these feet have hammered through dozens of hiking boots and running shoes, pushed through sprains and splinters and bursitis and blisters. All miles they've known are crushed into this single step.

In the very beginning, overbearing fatigue finally sent me to a rheumatologist in a tweed suit who gave me the first name—celiac sprue. Just stop eating gluten, he told me, and you'll be all better. I did, and as the weeks of adjustment added up, I found my energy buoying back up from some previously unknown depths. My digestive tract, blunted for years by antibodies churning out after my immune system mistook gluten for a foreign invader, softened and flattened to a normalcy I'd forgotten.

I wish that had been it. I wish the tweed-clad doctor had been right, to just stop eating gluten and all my problems would be over. But I also wish he'd ordered more tests like I asked him to when I returned six months later with symptoms creeping back in, or looked closer at my elevated and speckled antinuclear antibodies, which, as far as I can tell, don't have much to do with celiac disease. His diagnosis was an easy fix, but not the whole picture. Not by a long shot.

When I go back to doctors' offices, more and more often, they find something new. Another dot on the map—vocal cord disfunction, chronic iron-deficiency anemia, reactive airway. I'm not looking for quick fixes for problems I can circle on a diagram of my body. I'm gathering evidence of a much larger system falling apart.

The piece that breaks you doesn't have to be a smoke plume wide and dark as an anvil, or a glacier disappeared. A fire started on MacDonald Pass but never torched the eastern slopes that bunch in dry pine all the way to a few blocks from my childhood home. Every year the snowfields that crest the pass make hollows twenty feet deep, just as they did twenty years ago when my family came up here to dig caves into the snow. I haven't lived long enough to miss what flakes never fall.

•

In my later years of high school and early college, I spent summers tallying the slow creep of noxious weeds, foreign invaders to the Rockies, plants with steel-clamped taproots and bitter-waxed leaves and no environmental immune system with the ability to barrage the hell out of them. Despite my love for all green and breathing things, I learned to toe my boot into ashen rosettes, guillotine heads of daisies that decades ago someone brought from Europe thinking they'd go nicely beside a white picket fence.

This isn't about foreign invaders, though. We're talking about puzzle pieces suddenly flipped belly-up, numbers of every sort on the rise. An innocuous black beetle worming and gnawing into a tree's living body. The mountain pine bark beetle didn't come from anywhere except where it already is, evergreen shoulders of the Rockies, old as rainbow trout and sagebrush. Still, we use the words invasion, diseased, epidemic. It's easy to lose sight of the long view, the circumstances that trick notions of belonging.

Mountain pine bark beetles feed on a tree's cambium layer, its living tissue beneath rough bark. This is the soft flesh that transports water and nutrients from the roots up the trunk and into chlorophyll-packed needles, which in turn send sugar pulled from sunlight to all those hard-working cells. The beetles wriggle through gaps in the pine's armor, then chew their way into this soft vertical highway, carbo-loading and boring roadways of their own.

It's hardly a symbiotic relationship. But it's one tested by millennia, a cyclical back-and-forth where sometimes the beetles come out on top, sometimes the pines. Feeling mandibles chewing on their tissues, the tree pumps the boreholes full of pitch, akin to blood to a wound. Sticky clots force the seed-sized beetles again into open air. Most of the time. Sometimes there are too many beetles, a tree already weakened by heart rot or drought. Its system can't drive the beetles out fast enough, and they continue to gnaw loopy burrows and pockets for milk-white eggs.

If a pine loses this battle, it's not because the beetles managed to consume all its cambium. Rather, it's strangulation. Too many tunnels around and around the trunk until all the vessels carrying nutrients and water gurgle to a halt, until the roots invested in good granite earth are flushing their riches to nowhere.

But the pines have one final advantage over the beetles—they know better how to tough out Rocky Mountain winters. Come first hard freeze, the bark beetles start wiggling themselves into their woody caves where they're sheltered by the tree's own tissue. In their insect vessels, blood washes full of antifreeze, so that as the temperature eases into deep winter, the beetles dream in a chilled hibernation.

Up to a certain point. Below −30 degrees Fahrenheit, the antifreeze starts to fail, and beetles freeze in earnest. Long stretches of these cold snaps have been regulars to the Intermountain West as long as pines and their beetle predators. When temperatures cascade this low, bark beetle populations face massive die-offs. Millions of lodgepole and ponderosa will greet the next spring mostly unburdened by their gnawing pests.

The problem is it just doesn't get that cold anymore. Or if it does, it's a short burst. Rarer are the weeks-long stretches of bitter cold that send moose browsing in backyards, or before the bark beetles have time to nestle in their dens of sawdust. The pines' circulation systems can only do so much to drive out the insects. Without the aid of deep cold come wintertime, they begin to succumb, smothered to bronze.

I grew up in the sweetness of ponderosa bark and citric tinge of lodgepole pitch. And by the time I became aware that the environment is a dynamic thing that people can meddle in, all these forests of pine were blushing the color of rust. By the early 2000s winters stuck to their mild trend. Lodgepole woods sweeping down from the Divide were all the same age class, their parents hauled away decades ago in booms of timber and mining. No great fires had raced through the trees, and when bark beetle populations peaked, they found thousands of acres of underprepared pines and hardly enough cold to curb their numbers.

It's a messy destruction, all these timbered slopes the color of smeared blood. Too many tipping points, too few nights gaping of a cold you can taste. The beetles know only their hunger for sweet strips of pinewood. Who can fault them for knowing their place in the frosted web, for a greed that was never theirs in the first place?

•

"At least you have a name now," a friend offers. "It's like there's been something huffing and pacing outside your house. And now you can name it, know what to expect. You open the door, and there's a bear on your front porch."

Systemic, the whole scope. Lupus, from the same word in Latin, named for the triangular markings of a wolf's face. Erythematosus, from the Greek *eruthēma*, meaning reddening.

A bear, dark and round as the new moon, tracing some invisible path up-valley to a glacier's fringe. Bears are like humans, rare mammals that walk on the heels of their feet. Fight or flight varies individual to individual, and in all my years wandering in their footprints, I've never met a bear who showed any intent in harming me. This metaphorical one, with all her bluff charges and blows from claws meant for grubbing, is the first.

I find another new word—chilblains. Inflammation of vessels in the fingers and toes that causes a backlog of blood, hence the cherry-tight swelling. It often pairs with Raynaud's syndrome, a disease of swelling in arteries of the extremities, which often tails lupus. Welts rise white and tender. Skin glosses and continues to balloon. I learn the trigger is exposure to cold.

I greet the first cold snap of the year with wool socks and stubbornness, even as the joints in my feet ache with that iron-hot gnaw. I won't call it determination, which hums of a hollow valor. Winter runs promise relief from a body hellbent on dragging me downward. My newest technique has been to fight fatigue with fatigue. Here, now, is a reason for my heart to race, for muscles to tense, for my body to crave repose. I step into the cold knowing well that it might just spin me deeper into exhaustion, that by evening all I'll be able to do is hobble through a reddening clamp. Every forced stride I map these roots: dams in my vessels as well as the pines, a brokenness whose name is too tangled and cavernous for one breath. I am running out of unmeddled timberland.

IV. Lungs

This should be the point where the story stumbles to climax. Where I tell you about another fire, and the July day when a thread of lightning split onto the steep hillsides south of Beeskove Creek. How for a moment I was consumed with an unborn grief picturing the Rattlesnake Mountains, a gentle blue rise north of Missoula, charred to scuffed obsidian. Or how, days later, not a quarter mile into a work hitch as a wilderness ranger for the Forest Service, my muscles gave way to this blurry mourning, my windpipe dammed two desperate breaths, and I thought my heart would stop surrounded by fat huckleberries.

But these moments are always staggered. In stories we can wrap them up, drawing lines between points as if there's no havoc of topography between them. In the simple way of things, here's how it happened: two days before summer solstice my rheumatologist gave me a name meaning wolf that rattled my future to shards, and one month later the place where I'd learned to love my self and body caught fire, and five days after that all this emotional weight churned alive, spun into every rivulet keeping me alive, and became a physical weight that knocked me to earth. In this story the Rattlesnake would char with a necessary cleanse. The purpose of breakage would be to reassemble a new and complete whole. The answer would be melded with finality.

In reality I have only chronic mess. An electrocardiogram, chest x-ray, pulmonary function test, cardiac echo, dozens more vials of blood—only to find no solid explanation. After two years with no known crumb of gluten near my mouth, a second endoscopy shows the villi of my small intestine still moderately blunted and hoarding lymphocytes. Despite the title of lupus christened on my charts, my labs are ambiguous, and it could just as well take the form of Sjögren's syndrome or vague mixed connective tissue disease. The hydroxychloroquine churns my stomach, but I swallow a pill every morning with breakfast, counting down the months until its benefits are supposed to kick in.

But this is not the simple way of things. Not even close. If this is the final destination, a mountainside searing for the sake of metaphor, a body twenty-six years old trembling with certainty of death, then we are already lost. Fatigue burns to malaise to a curtain sodden with mud. A beetle wriggles through sawdust damp with January rain, and all it takes is one more rusted pine for the word epidemic to bloom. Chemicals gum the retina but so does every stencil of smoke on my horizon, tick marks of flare to a gathering fever. I've watched the reddening creep across my cheekbones, counted groans in a cold house as my feet swelled and throbbed in self-made frostbite, felt a borehole come full circle around my throat. I cannot explain the depth of this terror, a body choking itself. I cannot explain the depth of this anger.

In the Rattlesnake, the Forest Service bulldozes indirect lines atop Sheep Mountain, fells century-old Douglas firs and ponderosas for helicopter drop sites, rallies in hotshot and type II incident crews from across the country, and drains bucketload after bucketload from Beeskove Lake. The total dollars spent racks up to over four million. Then, after a few weeks, the incident crews pull out, the hotshots switch to rehab, and the Beeskove Fire, which never threatened structures and did little but meander dreamily towards the wilderness boundary, is left to burn naturally.

•

Humans, my dad sometimes says, are the aliens. The sickness. And it's an agreeable perspective when you watch species after species ticked off the extinction list, the Amazon blurred in smoke, seabirds tarred over their feathers, ice plateaus of Antarctica sloughing into open water only to crumble the permafrost banks of Newtok. Still, I think of corn, which is functionally barren without human hands. I think of the wildfires that soothed the Rockies long before my ancestors arrived here and changed all the names, fires ignited by people who knew fireweed and willow are good for elk and larch seedlings nestled in the dark loam. I think of the four years I spent working and wandering the Rattlesnake Mountains, a quiet cut of wildness, where my purpose was to smudge human footprints while sawing the trails clear for our wonder. I think of autoimmunity, which holds in its vocabulary the words relapse and remission, but not malignant or benign.

It comes back to the words. A felled tree, a decision made in a windowless room where ten years of spoils is worth it because you'll be dead in fifty. A misinterpretation of a holy book, toxic slag tainting groundwater and the voices who drink it silenced. A white blood cell deep in marrow suddenly struck with twisted purpose. Words strung together make a narrative, which is a weighted invisible, a thunderhead poised below the horizon, a city founded on the myth of a nurturing wolf, its namesake carved in haunts of white marble. It has no body except for the one it inhabits.

•

Once, this place knew glaciers.

The day after I thought my heart was going to stop itself, I sit for twelve hours on the hood of a Forest Service pickup turning back joggers and mountain bikers as they reach the Beeskove Fire closure. Every so often a string of hotshot buggies or fire rigs come rolling through, churning sepia dust into the slatted limbs of ponderosa and fir. Otherwise the hours are long and quiet. There's no smudge of smoke to be seen. Sea-jade algae flourish in fungi's elbows. A parade of ants steers clear of lingering diesel fumes.

The ranger district picked this spot for the closure because it's the branching point of various trails, a solid stopping point three miles from the trailhead and another three from the fire itself. But there's a grandness here too. The ants, I'm sure, know it, as do the lichen, the pines, the dark-eyed juncos, the lupine. Epochs banded in silt and clay beyond where the wind can reach, glints of quartz like starlight.

Glaciers shaped the valleys of the Rattlesnake Mountains during the last ice age. They left behind cirques, hanging and U-shaped valleys, including the main drainage of Rattlesnake Creek, which gathers itself in the shelved woods below the wilderness's highest peak and drapes downslope like a fishhook. A millennia ago it was only a cropped ravine, a fissure where ice pried with fingers of hoarfrost. The glacial tongue grew fat on long winters and followed the oldest rule of gravity. Like a bear to a grubbed log, it dug headfirst into the earth, breaking horizons free of their planes. Humus churned to bedrock, obsidian-glossed fossils reintroduced to the cold and oxygenated air. Season after season the glacier slipped from high-hanging lofts down its self-made passage. Then, having plowed a rim of sediment two hundred feet high at its front, it stopped, and warmed, and melted to the nurseries of bull trout.

I spend all day perched at the base of the glacial moraine terminus without giving it much thought. The sun's passage through bunches of pine needles feels long enough, and there's a weight still gnawing at my chest fit to align itself with the glacier's ghost. This is before all the serious tests, before I wheeze my lungs' atmosphere into a glass chamber, before I watch the valves of my heart flit open and shut on an ultrasound monitor. I return to work because my heart's still thumping, since that seems to be the black-and-white point of decision. A moment of free fall, of stubbornness.

Autoimmunity works like this. The self and the other blur. A sturdy branch of lung tissue turns to a knotted virus, a forest of villi clear-cut from the inside, beetles thick as sable blood. A bear, hungry with her promised winter, moves through the morning crepuscular. Take the long view, wind-struck on a summit and exposed to every direction. We forget the land has horizons that have nothing to do with hope. Here is a story, one thread on top of another, ash of the oldest trees and bones of a free-roaming bison. Poison and fencing and flagpoles and oil. All those words of possession and salvation. I've panned for silver linings and found only chaos, wept these questions whose meanings dart quick and brief as hummingbirds. How can you hate a broken body? Shout through the thinnest air of the alpine and the echo returns cuffed by snow and whitebark pitch—the same way you can hate a broken world.

Maybe it wasn't grief that tumbled me over, but the shock of all that beauty as it calved to disconnect. I'm not buried yet. Maybe there is strength in the mess—not how my lungs once rushed like Chinook winds, but the way this absence hangs between my ribs, a moraine that didn't slough away, a glacier gone, a quiet fire in its place.

Acknowledgments

First and foremost I would like to thank Natasha Trethewey and everyone at *River Teeth* for the honor of selecting this collection for the 2022 Literary Nonfiction Book Prize. I am also deeply grateful to everyone at University of New Mexico Press for their time and commitment in turning my manuscript into a beautiful published work.

Thank you to those from my time at the University of Montana, where I first discovered my love of nonfiction environmental writing: Robert Stubblefield, Laurie Yung, Phil Condon, Nicky Phear, and everyone in the Wilderness and Civilization Program.

This collection simply would not be here without my cohort and community of writers at Chatham University, especially those who workshopped "Exposure," "Siento," and "What Stones Hold." Our time together is a warm weight on my shoulder every time I write. Thank you in particular to Aspen for your shared love of landscape and wonder in this messy world, and Lee, Shelby, Amanda, Mel, Cedric, Mike, and Elia. I am deeply grateful for the mentorship and guidance from Marc Nieson, Sheila Squillante, Melanie Fox, and Sheryl St. Germain.

To my colleagues on the Missoula Ranger District and Beartooth Ranger District, thank you for your patience and camaraderie in working in wild places, even with the ticks and long damp days. Thank you especially to Melanie for all our lady-crew adventures, and to Tom for your compassion during the heartbreak of my final season. I'm endlessly grateful to Al Hilshey for your mentorship and deep knowledge of the Rattlesnake Wilderness, from our first trip to Little Lake to our ascent of McLeod Peak together.

There are so many individuals who have supported me and my writing to get to this point—my grandparents and brother Sean, friends from all stages of my life, and strangers and family who hosted me on all my ramblings. To Courtney, you beautiful land mermaid, these pages wouldn't be bound without your friendship and belief in me. To my partner, Court, your support and love means the wild,

wild world to me. And to my parents, I will never be able to thank you enough for all your encouragement of my writing, for teaching and modeling for me what it means to explore, know, care, and fight for our shared wild places, from the alpine tundra of the Beartooths to the weed-cracked sidewalks of Love Canal. You were my first trail companions, my first storytellers, and the best I could ask for.

Finally, thank you to Ana Maria Spagna, a mentor in both my writing as well as what it means to be a queer woman on the trail. In February of 2020 we met in Missoula's Butterfly Herbs to talk about this very collection, and you were the one to suggest submitting it to *River Teeth*'s Literary Nonfiction Book Prize. I was four months unemployed from my dream job, depressed, alienated from my body and sense of place, and unsure if this book was even me anymore. Maybe it's okay that it's not, you told me, and that's the way forward. You gave me a blessing to grieve that I didn't know I needed, that I have never let go.

Versions of some of the essays in this collection originally appeared in the following publications:

Bright Bones: Contemporary Montana Writing: "Headwater"
Camas: "Exposure"
CutBank: "Places to Avoid at Dusk"
Flyway: "Porcupine Ridge"
The Hopper: "Reasons to Carry Bear Spray"
The Normal School: "Siento"
Orion: "The Long View"
Secret Destinations: Chatham University MFA Field Seminar Writings: "What Stones Hold"

I am deeply grateful for the readers and editors of these magazines, journals, and books for shaping and giving a first home to these pieces.

References

The following material is quoted or paraphrased in this book:

Baldwin, James. *Giovanni's Room*. New York: Vintage Books, 1956.

Chaney, Rob. "Loose moose prompt Rattlesnake trail closures." *The Missoulian*, March 5, 2019. https://missoulian.com/news/local/loose-moose-prompt-rattlesnake-trail-closures/article_b4543001-fb3d-562a-9d37-74923313988c.html.

Prine, John. "Angel from Montgomery." *John Prine*. Atlantic Records, 1971.

Schrödinger, Erwin. "The present situation in quantum mechanics." Translated by John D. Trimmer. *Proceedings of the American Philosophical Society* 124, no. 5 (1980): 323–38. http://www.jstor.org/stable/986572.